Dedication

We affectionally dedicate this book to all of the working women who wonder why they don't make a LA-Z-GIRL recliner and to all of the men who think that PMS is an airline.

I'm OK...But You Have a Lot of Work To Do !

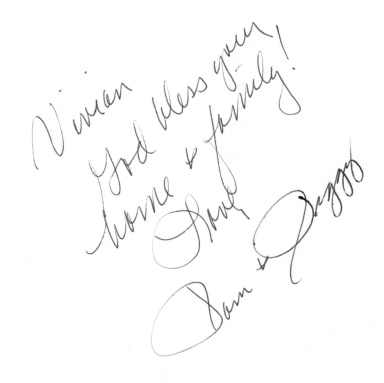

Vivian
God bless your home & family!
Love
Sam & [signature]

I'm OK...But You Have a Lot of Work To Do !

By
Pam Young
and
Peggy Jones

Published by
Permanent Press Washington
for
Sidetracked Home Executives, Inc.

Sidetracked Home Executives® Edition

Copyright © 1989
  by Pamela I. Young and Peggy A. Jones

Permanent Press Washington
401 N.W. Overlook Drive
Vancouver, Washington 98665

Permanent Press Washington is a
Sidetracked Home Executives® Company

Printed in the United States of America
First Printing: April 1989

Book and cover design by Pam Young and Peggy Jones

Illustrations by Jim Shinn

Library of Congress Cataloging in Publication Data
Young, Pam.
I'm OK...But You Have a Lot of Work To Do!
1. Self Help/Humor.   2. Husbands.   3. Time Management.
I.   Jones, Peggy.
89-91079
ISBN 0-9622475-0-2 (U.S.A.)

Acknowledgments

We want to thank the two men in our lives, Danny and Terry, but there aren't words meaningful enough (not even in the synonym finder) to express the depth of our gratitude.

When we couldn't convince anyone in the publishing world that this book had any value, their support and encouragement gave us the confidence to self-publish. That decision could not have been made without their emotional, physical and financial backing. In addition to all of that, their input throughout our writing gave us a balanced perspective and caused this book to be one that men will enjoy as much as women.

We want to give special thanks to each of our children:

Mike, Peggy, Joanna, Chris, Jeff and Allyson, for their willingness to be guinea pigs for our project.

We also want to thank Chris for letting us invade his bedroom each day to use his very personal computer. His generosity in sharing his property (paid for with two years of lawn-mowing money) allowed us to finish this book several months sooner than we had expected. (We have written three books, using pencils and tablet paper, and this new invention makes us also grateful to the folks at Commodore.)

At the risk of sounding like an Academy Awards acceptance speech, we must thank our parents for raising us to believe that success comes from having a positive attitude, even in negative circumstances.

Growing up, we were allowed to be discouraged, depressed, angry or in a bad mood, but Mom was always there with a timer and we had ten minutes to get through it and get on with life. The timer has come in handy during the evolvement of this project.

Dee Anne Cloke, our assistant for ten years, and personal friend for twenty, was instrumental in making us know that the information in this book would work in other families besides ours. Her husband, Dan, we are pleased to report, now makes his own lunch, cooks from time to time, buys groceries and does laundry, dishes and the vacuuming! Dee Anne's opinion as a wife and mother is invaluable to everything we do. Her prayers have been felt and appreciated from the beginning.

Our wonderful friend, Kac Young, deserves special thanks for her daily, long-distance hotline of quality feedback. She has been a great cheerleader for this book, but just as valuable, she has had the courage to tell us when something didn't work. We have always respected her professional advice, but her personal friendship is priceless.

Thanks to Fredda Isaacson, Vice President and Senior Editor at Warner Books. We were elated that she loved our manuscript because her personal and editorial opinion is most highly respected.

We also wish to thank Warner Books. We were privileged to have had them as our publisher for the last several years.

We want to thank Jim Shinn for agreeing to do the art work in the book, in spite of his busy schedule. We have worked with Jim on other projects and continue to be amazed at his talent. With only brief descriptions for each drawing, his imagination and sense of humor come to life in the collection of cartoons in this book.

Special thanks to our editor, Sydney Craft Rozen, for once again saving us from literary embarrassment. To have Sydney help us, over the last ten years and four books, has been a real blessing. Her unique ability to edit a manuscript, without changing the voice of the author, is rare and truly appreciated.

Thanks to all of the librarians at the Fort Vancouver Regional Library, who continually offer their services, whether they research a name, locate a book on short notice or find a telephone number.

We are especially grateful to Kate McKern, the producer of "A.M. Northwest," Portland's live television talk show, for her enthusiasm for this book. Thanks to Bob Bullock for the photograph that appears on the back cover of our book. Thanks again to our friends (and the hosts of A.M. Northwest), Jim Bosley and Mary Starrett, for always making us feel at home.

Thanks to Carole Collins for her walking company each morning. Laughing with Carole was a great way to start the day. We miss her.

Pam especially thanks Bill and Deborah Brock for a week in San Diego. Free of the rat race at home, she was able to write non-stop in a luxurious hotel, interrupted only by room-service trays and an occasional dip in the pool.

Peggy especially thanks Therese Ahlberg for brainstorming with her to help pick the perfect title for the book. Even though we weren't able to use her favorite entry, "The Clutter Posse," she was influential just the same. And thanks to Douglas and Jeanne Jurgens, (Photography with Our Special Touch) for their very special ability to capture a close family feeling and a nice expression on five different faces.

Thanks to our friend, Roger Sullivan (B. Dalton Books, Vancouver Mall) for always acting as a sounding-board for what he thinks will be popular on the bookshelves. From the first book we wrote, Roger has helped us with marketing, and we will always be indebted to him.

In memory of Mr. Tom Binford, (Binford and Mort Publishing), we are grateful for all that he taught us about the publishing business. Without his guidance years ago, we would not have been confident enough to self-publish this book today.

Thanks to Kathy Wright, our personal banker and even more personal friend. Kathy can process a loan with her hands tied behind her back. With flowers on her desk, rings on her fingers and always enough time for her customers, her vivacious, fun-loving presence makes our bank the friendliest financial institution in Vancouver.

Thanks to Linda Haines, who has been with us for many years, helping us get things finished and contributing her beautiful spirit to our little office. Without her extra help when this book came down to the press roll, we would be in a home somewhere.

Thanks to Dick Hands, who helped us with his expertise in the publishing business, borrowed our yardstick to make sure the book was the right size and played receptionist for us at the same time.

Thanks to the lady who wrote to us after we were on the Geraldo show and warned us not to get mean.

Thanks to John Boswell, our agent, for his sincere good

wishes for our success with this book.

We want to thank our friends at Print & Publish; Joyce Beaman for her encouragement throughout this project, and especially (in memory) her very special husband, John, who showed us new possibilities in publishing, cutting our costs in half. We also appreciate Judy McGregor, for her keen eye and fast fingers. Working with such nice people has been a real pleasure.

Finally, thanks to all of the wonderful women who bought this book before it was even printed, helping us to know that there was a market for it.

Table of Contents

Prologue

With all the stress involved in juggling two careers, have you ever asked yourself, "Is it worth it?"

<u>DISILLUSIONED</u>

I got a job a month ago.
Today's the day they paid.
They took out some withholding
And FICA's got it made.
When I cashed my paycheck
For the thirty days of work,
I went to pick the children up
And nearly went berserk!
'Cause when I paid the person
Who agreed to watch my brood,
There was just enough left over
To buy the dog some food.

My wallet would be thicker.
I'd ease financial tension
And we'd no longer bicker
Over little things like overdrafts
And disconnected phones.
We'd pay off all our credit cards.
We'd reconcile our loans
On the car we bought in '83
And trashed in '85,
And the one we're driving currently
And hope it stays alive.

I thought that when I went to work
The checkbook would be in the black.
Maybe he'd buy that boat he loves
And I could take a whack
At tennis at the country club,
Where everybody goes.
I'd buy a BMW.
I'd get some classy clothes.
We'd take that cruise to Mexico,
The vacation of our dreams.
We'd leave the kids at Gramma's,
Romance bursting at the seams.

We'd rip up all the carpeting.
The walls could use some paint.
The kitchen needs remodeling;
The sink's my main complaint.
I'd get to buy a stereo
That plays a compact disc.
I'd also get a VCR.
That too is on my list.

The kids don't like the sitter.
My life is in a shambles.
I never see my husband,
And all we eat is Campbell's.
There isn't room for romance.
We're lucky if we kiss.
There's never time for leisure.
It's the simple life I miss.

All I ever wanted was
To ease financial stress.
Instead I'm hypertensive
'Cause the house is in a mess.

I guess I was mistaken
By what I thought would be.
There is no extra money,
And there's no time left for me.

If our poem sounds familiar, something has to change in your life! It doesn't matter what your job is, or whether you're disillusioned with it. If you work outside of your home, you need family cooperation! Before you end up talking to the people in your wallpaper, we hope you will stop what you've been doing and read this book.

Introduction

If you are anything like we are, you hate to waste your time reading the introduction of a book, because you are anxious to get to the first chapter.

Our literary agent said that we didn't need to worry about an introduction because you wouldn't buy this book in the first place. He said that a woman who has kids, a husband and a job outside of her home doesn't have time to read, and if she did, she'd rather be sleeping. If he's right about that, then you need this book more than any other, because it contains information that is vital to your sanity. You'll actually learn a clever yet incredibly simple solution to a very messy dilemma: lack of family cooperation at home.

This new way to get help from the people you live with

actually causes each member of the family to be account-able for his or her own messes, and <u>YOU</u> WILL NEVER NAG AGAIN!

This book is not just another how-to book. We didn't want it to be squeezed in between handbooks on stain removal and household hints, so we decided to give it a humorous and, we admit, slightly self-righteous title, hoping it will stack up next to Erma's homespun volumes of humor.

Although "I'm OK...But You Have a Lot of Work To Do!" was written to help the 75% of women in America who work outside of their homes and are still doing 97% of the housework and child care, the primary reason we spent 4,843 hours at the typewriter was for a higher purpose. We wanted to tap out something that would ultimately get men and women to laugh together while they work things out at home.

We all know that women are not going to get the cooperation they need from men by using the old feminine tricks of whining, manipulating, conniving and nagging. Butting egos with the opposite sex doesn't work, either. It's time to try a fresh approach, one that includes LOVE and LAUGHTER. One with a united motive: more time to spend with each other, loving, laughing and living in a home where there is peace, joy and order.

Now that you know what this book is about, let us give you a little background about ourselves. We are sisters from Vancouver, Washington. It seems that whenever we go anywhere east of Idaho and say we're from Vancouver,

Washington, no one hears the Washington part. Invariably, when we mention Vancouver, someone will flashback and swoon about spending their honeymoon there. Unless she and her bridegroom stayed at the Ferrymen's Inn off I-5, they have to be picturing Vancouver, British Columbia.

Once, during a tour to promote one of our books about home organization, we were interviewed by a reporter from a small Midwestern newspaper. When the story ran, the headline read: "Two Canadian Nuns Find Order." Not that it really matters, but just for the record, we are BLOOD sisters from the USA.

Twelve years ago, we decided to get organized. We were admitted slobs back then (we think it's genetic), and it was out of desperation that we made the choice to change. We had lost our self-esteem and faced losing our husbands. Our six children ranged in age from 16 months to 12 years. Soon after we "found order," we wrote our first book, "Sidetracked Home Executives". We wanted it to help homemakers who were disorganized by nature to get control over their lives.

At that time, only 22% of the women in America worked outside of their homes. Twelve years ago, we couldn't imagine working outside of ours (there was too much to do inside of them), and if we had wanted to get out there and work, we wouldn't have had a clue about what we would do.

When the Women's Liberation Movement began in the '60s, we really didn't relate to their grievances. While they were screaming for equal pay, we worked at jobs that didn't pay anything. While their extremists were out burning their bras, we were trying to squeeze a little extra money out of our grocery budgets to buy new ones.

Today we have joined the majority of women in our country who work at a job outside of the home. We are fortunate to own our own business, which gives us the freedom to put our families first. Ironically, we fell into the business world because we wrote books about our homes, and for the last 12 years, part of our work has been helping women to feel proud of the work they do as wives and mothers.

Usually mothers are too busy with mothering to realize what a huge job they have undertaken. We didn't begin to give ourselves credit for the most important work that anyone can do, until after the child-rearing project was almost completed.

It was just recently, while fooling around with a pocket calculator, that we were shocked to discover what we had accomplished over the last two decades. Collectively, we had been homemakers for 44 years, and in that time we had almost finished raising six children. We'd been pregnant for 54 months and had been in labor 52 hours. We'd produced more than 8,000 gallons of mother's milk, sewn more than seven miles of fabric and baked more than 48,000 chocolate chip cookies.

We calculated that we had changed 78,840 diapers, and when Peggy's husband, Danny, heard that figure, he challenged us. "Hey, wait a minute! Aren't you guys exaggerating a little? What do you do, change 'em after every meal? That'd be three diapers a day!"

Peggy was quick to set him straight. "No, Danny, wake up and smell the hamper! First of all, babies eat more than three times in 24 hours, and you'd know they use more than three diapers a day if you'd changed a few of them." His apathy wasn't surprising. He really thought PMS was an airline. (Peggy still hasn't been able to explain that one to him. He just thinks she's a frequent flyer.)

When we were finished with our statistics, we were impressed with what we'd accomplished. Our calculations gave motherhood a new perspective.

We know that our lives are quite average. Before we came up with the ideas we share in this book, we were stretched so far that we were as tight as a pair of size "A" pantyhose would be on a professional basketball player. Although we were in business together outside of our homes, we were still doing most of the cooking, cleaning and laundry. We were picking up after everybody, too. When our children got hurt, or hungry or wanted to show off something they were proud of, they'd come to us. The animals followed us, the school called us, the dentist and the doctor reminded us of our families appointments, and, when it came to entertaining and special holidays...it was all up to us.

We were also frustrated because the men in our lives had no idea of the extent of our work load. They were

brought up to think that housework is women's work. Their mothers never taught them how to mend seams, iron shirts, shuck corn or plan Christmas. They thought that their fair share of domestic responsibility was taking care of the yard and the family car. (They never stopped to think how often they change the oil, compared to how often they change their underwear.)

We carried the full responsibility for the way our houses looked. We were the ones who were constantly ordering everybody around. Consequently, we were not the most popular members of our families. We nagged until we turned magenta trying to get the cooperation we wished would come automatically.

We know that one of the biggest problems a woman faces today is juggling the responsibilities of her home and family, and the pressures of a job outside of her home. Since we had been struggling with the same dilemma, even after writing three books on how to GET ORGANIZED, we knew that most women were having a hard time. We had also figured out that the MAIN problem was lack of cooperation from capable family members. Our challenge was to figure out how to motivate that vast pool of untapped energy into sharing the domestic work load.

Our first thought was to try to come up with a game that would encourage cooperation. Could we compare cleaning the toilet to landing on Boardwalk? Would a husband be willing to shake a pair of dice to see if he had to go to jail or vacuum the living room? Would a family that had been oblivious to the work load in a home, suddenly thrill to play a game that would inevitably get each person to do his or her share of the upkeep of the house? If we could think up a game that, when our family members played it, they'd be cleaning the house, we would have our hands on a gold mine. We would be able to help women everywhere win the losing battle of clutter, chaos and lack of cooperation.

Make a game of housework! Let's see, we could call it Cooperation. Everyone would sit at the table with the old Monopoly board. Each player would pick from an assortment of tiny cleaning tools: a toilet brush, a broom, a dust pan, etc. Starting on "Go" with several hundred dollars in play money, a player would roll the dice and move his vacuum cleaner the right amount of spaces.

If he landed on "Marvin Gardens," maybe he would have to go pull weeds. If he moved to the "B&O Railroad," he'd go out and wash the car. Landing on "Park Place" would mean we'd have him polish the silver. Of course, he could pay somebody else to do it, but he'd have to watch his money, because every time he'd pass "Go," he'd need to have enough cash to buy more cleaning supplies.

When a player had cleaned three of the same colored properties, he would get a janitorial contract for that group, and if anyone landed on him, they would have to pay a designated cleaning fee. If a player had to "Go to Jail," he'd have to clean the garage or the basement. Whenever he landed on "Free Parking," he'd have to go to an Amway meeting.

The "Community Chest" cards would contain Heloise-type cleaning hints, stain removal instructions and party clean-up cards. The "Chance" cards would take care of nasty messes like "Hose out the garbage can," "Clean out the kitty litter box" or "Your dog just threw up on your white carpet. If you didn't purchase the right cleaning products when you went around 'Go,' pay each player 400 dollars."

Ha ha. If anyone in either of our families thought a game would entail work, they wouldn't want to play. It would be easier to draft a board game called Procrastination. It would have all the little trinkets Cooperation had, only instead of miniature cleaning utensils, there would be a couch, a bed, a recliner, a bar stool and a hammock to choose from.

The players would have to count out a bunch of play money and divide up the sleeping, loafing and lounging cards. Players would spend a minimum of 45 minutes looking all over the house for the rules and missing pieces to the game, such as the dice and colored plastic tiddlywinks that the manufacturer never got around to putting in the box in the first place. Then, after the pre-game preparations, the family would leave the game on the table and go watch TV.

We could see our kids liking Procrastination, but a game called Cooperation? Why would anyone want to play? They wouldn't!

What we did ultimately figure out, was a way to get the entire family to WANT to cooperate and accept their share of the household responsibilities! Once your family accepts the idea, things will change OVERNIGHT and, as we said earlier, you'll never nag again!

Before we let the miracle out, we would like to invite you to come into our homes and see what led up to our discovery.

I'm OK...But You Have a Lot of Work To Do !

Chapter One:

The Inside Story

Hazel Dell, Washington, (a sleepy community established in a hazelnut orchard, three miles north of Vancouver), inside the home of Peggy Jones. March 24, 1987

Six a.m. I woke up to the cheerful voices of my sister and her walking friends, as they passed by my house on their daily four-mile hike. I rolled over and looked at my mate. Danny's mouth was slightly open as he snored softly, his morning breath gently puffing into my face every six seconds. Not ready to stir, I adjusted my breathing so that our exhales matched. I stood it as long as I could.

"Time to get up, Danny," I graveled.

"Huh?"

"Time to get up. The walkers just went by. It's six."

"Okay..."

"Danny, do you think we should start walking?"

"Where?" He yawned and stretched at the same time.

"With Pam's group. It sounds like they have a lot of fun. Look at us. We're still in bed. Don't you feel guilty, lying here? By the time we get up, they've done their exercise for the day. What do we do? We sleep as late as we possibly can.

"I worry about us now that we're forty. You know how high your cholesterol was two years ago... Well, I'll bet it's gone up. I'm going to make an appointment for you to get it checked. Pam says we should be drinking more water, too. At Weight Watchers, they told her everybody needs to drink at least eight glasses a day. We need to do that...So what do you think?"

"Yeah, I'll have a glass of water."

"No, I mean, what do you think about walking? I know it's not something you're just dying to do, but look at them. It started out with just Anne Skordahl and her neighbor, then Anne asked Carole and Carole asked Pam. Then Les started going because he was worried about the Hazel Dell rapist getting Carole, and now the Yearouts (you know Orville and Alberta)...Danny?...Danny! Danny, do you think we should start walking?" There was no answer from him so I answered myself, "Yeah, maybe in the summer when it warms up."

The morning started out the same as any other busy weekday. Five people, all getting ready to leave the house at the same time, caused the usual chaos. The bathrooms were taken by the two teenagers, and the kitchen showed signs of a hurried breakfast, but this morning was unusually tense. I had been out of town for a couple of days, to tape some television spots with my sister, and the family was feeling the effects of my absence.

"Babe, are we out of shampoo?" Danny called to me from the shower.

"Just a minute!" I dashed to the supply cupboard in the hall. I was used to shopping in bulk at Cram-co (it was really called Costco, but we renamed it because we could never cram all we bought into the car), so I was sure I would find an extra gallon of shampoo. I rummaged through the surplus inventory of products. I found three economy size cans of industrial strength bathroom cleaner, two gallons of Windex, a tub of Epsom Salts, six Comet cleansers (in institutional-size cans), a pound of Q-tips, a pound of Band-Aids, a quart of Liquid Woolite, two aerosol cans of hair spray (for professional use only) and a half gallon of Scope.

I flew to my suitcase, thinking there might be some shampoo left in a travel container I'd taken on the trip. I pawed through the clothes and found the plastic bottle. It was empty.

"Peggy! Are you getting the shampoo or what? I'm running out of hot water!" Danny's voice was urgent.

As was often the case throughout my genetically disorganized life, my right brain kicked in and came to the rescue. I ran back to the supply cupboard, grabbed the Liquid Woolite and filled the little bottle.

"Here you go, Babe. Use this. I guess it's time for me to make a run over to Cram-co again."

Pam and I always enjoyed our seasonal trips to the big wholesale warehouse in Portland. Even though we could never get out of there for under two hundred dollars, somehow we knew we HAD to be saving money. Going across the Columbia River into Oregon made us feel like pioneer women, teaming up the wagon and driving into town to get provisions for the winter. We called ourselves Lois and Clark. I was making the bed when Danny came in with a towel wrapped around him. "Boy, does that shampoo ever suds up! I had trouble rinsing it out."

"Hmm..." I didn't look at him. I went on making the bed. "How come you never make the bed, Danny?"

"'Cause you do."

"If I didn't make it, would you?'

"I don't know. Probably not. What have I got to wear, Babe?"

"I don't know. I've been gone. Did you get your clothes from the cleaners?"

"I wasn't aware you'd taken them in."

"I took them before I left."

"Well, that doesn't do me a lot of good right now, does it?" His face glared down into mine.

I was just about to say, "Now wait a minute, pal. Who made me your slave?" when Danny pivoted to go to his closet and fell into my open suitcase. "Did you have any plans to unpack this thing or were you just going to leave it out here on the rug.?" He wouldn't accept help getting out of the suitcase, and waved me out of his way. "I'm gonna be late for work. Just see if you can put an outfit together for me, would you?"

He hurried to the bathroom, and I heard the hair dryer go on. I looked in his closet and scrounged up an exhausted ensemble. It was obvious he needed new clothes. That wasn't my fault, I reassured myself. After all, he had been a uniformed policeman for the last couple of years and his new job in Investigations had recently put him in plain clothes. Unfortunately, his wardrobe was skimpy and out-dated. His aversion to fitting rooms and tailors had kept him away from the mall.

"Peggy!" Danny yelled from the bathroom. "Can you catch the back of my hair? I can't get it to stay down."

I rushed in to help him. He looked like one of the Three Stooges. Who would think that hair and wool wouldn't be the same? I took the brush from Danny and made a futile attempt to calm the coif.

"I think you blew it dry wrong. I'm afraid it doesn't want to go down."

Danny grabbed the professional hair spray and gave his head a good going-over. Then he took the brush and tried to force the follicles into place. They stuck together in wet clumps. I put the hand mirror back in the drawer.

"How does it look in back?" It looked worse than I had ever seen it look in 20 years. "Fine," I said, hoping he'd take my word for it. After all, what were his options...wash it over again and this time use Joy or Sergeant's Flea and Tick Shampoo, wear a hat, or call in sick? There were no options.

Danny stormed back into the bedroom. I shoved the suitcase under the bed, out of his way. He threw on the stupid outfit I had laid out for him. The slacks were about an inch too short (shrunken victims of too many tumbles in the Whirlpool), but he was moving so fast, it was hard to notice. I followed him as he started to leave. "See you tonight." He dutifully kissed me, a quick, off-centered smack, and started through the front door.

Our two German shepherds had been on one of their all-night digs, and there was a huge pile of dirt from the planter on the first step of the porch. Danny's long, rubber-like legs absorbed the surprise of running up and over the mound of dirt, and he recovered gracefully as he negotiated the hill like a flamingo.

"I'll get this cleaned up, Danny. You go on to work...Don't forget to drink your water."

"My water?"

"Your water. Remember, Sissy says you're supposed to drink eight glasses every day?"

He muttered something I didn't care to ask him to repeat, and he was off to fight crime.

I went back into the house, making a mental note to get a shovel as soon as the kids left for school.

"Did you make my lunch, Mom?" Chris, my 15-year-old, asked. He was pouring himself a glass of apple juice.

"No. Get a dollar out of the money drawer."

"There's nothing in there," Jeff, 14, said. "I already looked."

"Where's my purse?"

We started hunting.

"Look under those newspapers, or maybe it's under that pile of clean clothes. Somebody go look in the car.

"Whose cereal bowl is this? Allyson, is this your bowl?"

"No, I didn't get any cereal. All the boxes in the pantry are empty."

"What!? Who keeps doing that? Don't put the box back in the cupboard if it's empty. How many times do I have to tell you guys, you don't put empty boxes back in the pantry? If the box is empty, put it in the trash!"

"Mom, will you tell Chris to quit hogging all the hot water? He was in the shower for 15 minutes!"

"I was not.

"Were too."

"Was not"

"Knock it off, you guys!"

"Here's your purse, Mom. I found it in the car." Ally tossed it on the counter and started to leave.

"Oh, good. Here, Chris, here's a five. You and Jeff stick together at lunch and bring me back my change. Put the jug of apple juice back, Chris. Ally, come and get your lunch money. Jeff, clean up your mess in the bathroom before you leave."

"Mom, can you go on a field trip with my class next Wednesday? My teacher says the snakes aren't out yet." Allyson, my sixth grader, was waving a permission slip at me.

"Snakes! Where are you going?!"

"To the Ridgefield Wildlife Refuge."

"Oh, no, Ally, I can't do that! The teacher promised me there wouldn't be any snakes the year I went with Jeff's class, and they were everywhere! I had to be carried back to the bus. It was humiliating! I'm surprised Ms. Mc-Eachron would even ask!"

"Mom, there's swimming after school and I have to work tonight. Can you wash my uniform? It's on the floor in my closet."

"I'll try. You'd better bring it upstairs and put it in the

39

hall so I don't forget. Bring up your other laundry, too. You guys need to do that every morning so I know how much there is to do."

Jeff came in the house after feeding the dogs. "Oh, Mom, you aren't going to like this. You should see the pool! The dogs went swimming and it's all muddy!"

"Great. Your dad will be thrilled to see that! Come on, you guys, you're going to miss the bus."

When the last one had gone out the door, I slumped down onto the couch. My life was not running smoothly.

I knew what I wanted it to be like. I wanted a modern-day Walton's Mountain, only with more money, a housekeeper and no in-laws living with me.

The children would adore each other, and honor and respect their father and me. They'd be so used to helping that I could say, "Go do your chores," and they'd know exactly what I meant by that. Our home would be clean, cozy and full of laughter, and we'd all look forward to worshipping together on Sundays.

Each morning I'd go to my warm, sunny kitchen and make the coffee. The children would make their own breakfast and, one by one, they'd rinse their dishes and cheerfully put them in the dishwasher. The sink and counters would be spotless, inviting me to start preparing a few things for dinner.

The pace would be unhurried, but steady, as each one

40

would shower and dress (in outfits they'd set out the night before). They'd make their beds, sort their laundry and get ready to leave for school.

As the last one stepped happily onto the school bus, Danny and I would linger over a tender good-bye kiss at the front door. Then I would enjoy a second cup of coffee in my peaceful, lovely living room, as I curled up with a good book. At the end of a chapter or two, I would check the soup in my crockpot and jump into a nice, hot shower.

I would put on a size-seven pair of stylish jeans and a crisp cotton blouse, step into a sporty pair of tennis shoes, put on coordinating earrings, fix my hair and do my makeup and, with an hour to kill before work, I'd check the 3x5 housekeeping cards in my home-organization kit. I'd set aside jobs for the housekeeper and do a bit of light housework myself. With soft music on the stereo, I'd rinse out a few hand-washables, shine the glass-top coffee table, set out the china for dinner and freshen the guest room.

Then my sister would come over to work on our novel.

"Mmmm...It sure smells good in here," she'd say.

"Really? It's probably the stuffing I made for the Cornish game hens, or maybe it's the soup simmering."

"Well, it smells wonderful"

We'd work until noon, do lunch at The Alexis, drop by our office to get our mail and knock off at three.

I would return to my home-sweet-home, and the aroma

of a delicious dinner would melt away any stress I'd collected.

My happy children would come home from school, and over a nice, tall glass of iced tea, they would share their day with me.

Danny would call to see if he could run any errands for me on his way home from work. The children would ask what they could do to help with dinner.

At 5 p.m., my husband would spring through the door and hand me a small bouquet of wild violets he'd picked. He'd put his arms around me and say, "These reminded me of you. You're so delicate that a good wind would blow you away!"

Then we'd sit out on the deck in matching chaise longues and, while sipping a fragrant glass of lemonade, we'd tell each other about our fabulous day.

We would enjoy our meal together as a family, and afterward, each one would wash his or her own dishes. Then Danny would insist that I relax and read the paper, while he and the children scoured the pots and pans, polished the sinks and wiped counters, damp-mopped the kitchen floor and emptied the garbage.

Unfortunately, Walton's Mountain was only a fantasy. The only mountain close to my house was Mount St. Helens!

Meanwhile...

Salmon Creek, Washington, (a sleepier community about three miles north of Hazel Dell), outside the home of Pam Young. March 24, 1987:

I got back from my sunrise trudge with a heavy heart to match my thighs. My friend, Carole, and I had started walking after weighing up the Christmas pounds we'd put on. To date, we figured we had walked about 320 miles, and we still hadn't lost a gram. Carole had even gained a pound more than what she had weighed the night she waddled into a Weight Watchers meeting, threw herself onto the stage and cried, "HELP ME!" She had even resorted to wearing what she termed her Watergate wardrobe. She said it consisted of several full cut garments that covered up everything.

I had started to gradually disappear into a cushion of cellulite when I stopped dating a mid-life jogger. It had been a relief to slow down from the fast lane at the athletic club. Now I was blessed with a man who had a rowing machine stored in his attic, and whose idea of exercise was bringing it down for his annual garage sale and hauling it back up afterward.

Back in January when I had bumped into Carole at the grocery store (we were both reaching for the same pork roast), it had been like running into myself in the mirror. We were the same age, height and weight, and we had identically proportioned bodies.

"Carole, how are you? I haven't seen you since...."

"Since that time we had lunch and ended up going out to dinner after that."

"Gad, how long ago was that?"

As we blocked the aisle, catching up on each other's activities, there was silent recognition that we had each put on a little weight. (We confided, later, that we had both felt a rush of grocery-cart guilt, until we realized that our purchases had been similar in their fat content.)

"Oh, Carole, I've gained ten pounds since Thanksgiving! I've just got to get a hold of myself! The trouble with me is that I'm self-indulgent. That's all there is to it. Look at the calories in this cart! I mean, please, I know I shouldn't have real butter and mayonnaise, and those cookies....I don't even remember putting them in there."

"Hey, self-indulgence is my middle name. I'll be at home all alone, minding my own business, and I'll think...***Hmmm, what sounds good?*** and before I know it, I've answered myself...***Well, how 'bout some ice cream?***...and then I think, ***You don't want it blank! Let's put some chopped cashews, a little chocolate syrup and Cool Whip on top!***' There's a little Mr. Sweet Tooth inside of me and he's a real hog!"

44

"What are we going to do?"

"Well, I started walking last week. I go four miles a day with Anne and Claudia. You oughta come along."

I joined the walkers, but here I was, three months and 320 miles later, still heavy. My only solace was that if I HADN'T exercised, I'd probably weigh ten pounds more than I did now.

As I reached my house, it didn't help my cloudy spirit to see the contents of my garbage can strewn all over the drive-way. My front yard looked like a landfill. I was embarrassed, especially since I'd written three books on getting organized, and I knew that this mess would delight Mrs. Dorchester, the neighborhood jogging gossip. Her network of rumor mongers always enjoyed finding any evidence to show that I needed to take some of my own advice.

As I picked up the junk in the yard, I thought about what had happened to me since Peggy and I had become organized 12 years earlier. We'd traveled all over the country, helping homemakers improve their domestic affairs. Things had definitely improved for me too, but they were far from perfect. I was still plagued, and probably always would be, with the effects of my genetic disorder...no left brain.

The garbage was a good example. The lid on the can had been squashed flat in the winter of '82 (it was buried under the snow when I ran over it with the car), but instead of buying a whole new can, I always balanced the useless lid on top of the contents of the over-stuffed garbage container.

Consequently, every garbage day there was a race to see who would get to my refuse first, Vancouver Sanitary Service or the neighbor's dog, Cody (a garbage and Labrador retriever mix).

In recent years, I'd had some drastic changes occur in my life (two of my children had gone away to college). Now, even more distressing, they both had returned home for spring break!

Joanna, 14, my born-organized child, and I had become quite comfortable without the chaos that her two genetically disorganized siblings could generate. When they returned, the house submerged under the clutter before I realized what had happened.

With the yard cleaned up, I vowed to get a new garbage can lid (I wondered if I could buy the top without the bottom), and I went into the house.

As I opened the door, Chelsea Marie, my basset hound puppy, greeted me with what had been one of my good high heels. I lobbed it in the vicinity of her toy box, which was filled with an assortment of objects she had, out of boredom, confiscated and destroyed. It contained a colorful variety of leather shoe casualties, a fuzzy assortment of the children's prized, stuffed animals that they had collected over the years, and a potpourri of things we'd neglected to put away.

The mark of a teething puppy was everywhere. I needed a basset hound like I needed a horse in the house, but Peggy

Ann, my 19-year-old, had bought her for me, knowing I'd always loved the breed. The puppy had been a surprise on my birthday. Peggy Ann had tied a big red bow around her neck. The message on the card said: "T.G.T.K.O.S.S.C.H.S. and M". (The Gift That Keeps On Smelling, Slobbering, Chewing, Howling, Shedding And Messing.) All the bother and all the mess was Puppy Chow under the bridge. I'd fallen madly in love with her.

Walking into the living room, I remembered there were four extra bodies staying over. Fraternity brothers of Mike's, my oldest offspring, were conked out in their clothes on the living room floor like a gathering of park-bench bums. Their party remains were everywhere. A rented movie was still in the VCR, and I cringed at the titles of the other two on the top of the T.V. I didn't care to know the name of the one they had fallen asleep to. I reminded myself that they were all over 21.

The morning-after kitchen was testimony to a great night before. The refrigerator was stripped of everything edible, including some borderline potato salad and a bowl of leftover beans that no one had liked in the first place. The home-movie goers had obviously enjoyed my absentee hospitality. (I had gone out to dinner and to a movie, then had slipped to bed while the Delta Upsiloners were engrossed in their video rentals.) Since it was only 8:15, I decided to let them sleep, while I took a shower and started polishing my half of an article Peggy and I had to finish for McCall's Magazine.

On the way to my desk in the corner of the living room, I tripped on the arm of one of the sleepers. He didn't move. *If the children's father still lived here, God forbid, these people would not be sacked out in my living room like this. We would have come home last night and he would have clicked off the TV and thrown a huge fit over the mess.*

I could feel my body start to tense, thinking of the scene that would have occurred if Mike's father lived here. I knew from experience that I hated confrontations like that. Still, I knew that as soon as these vacationing scholars stirred, I would have to tell them how upset I was with the way my living room and kitchen looked. I knew it would be a hassle to get them to clean everything up. Since I hate situations where I have to be the "bad guy," I didn't relish the inevitable clash.

I wish there was a man I could hire to come over and throw a fit for me. I would leave for an hour and, when I came back, everything would be straightened out. I'd find his ad in the yellow pages:

"ATTENTION, SINGLE MOMS: Sgt. Stickler will take care of all disciplinary actions in your home. I will put an end to unnecessary bickering, enforce punishments, make rules and deliver lectures approved by the mother. Hourly rate or salary. Call 574-MEAN and I'll wear the pants in your family!"

I looked at the rough draft of the article we were writing. "Fifteen Hassle-Free Ways to Get Your Family to Help Around the House."

I glanced back at the living room, *How can I possibly contribute to this article when my home looks like a mission house on skid row? I'd do better, writing about the hazards of being a single parent. At least I'd be writing about what I know! The 15 million women like me would probably love to read about somebody else who has had to raise her children by herself.*

I had assumed full responsibility for my three kids when they were four, nine and twelve. Their father had moved to California after the divorce, and I was left to raise them without the power that comes when two parents stand together against the constant challenge of growing children. So many times I had wished that I could say, "You'll have to ask your dad," or "Wait until your father gets home." Instead, I was the only one there to help them through the tangle of thoughts and feelings of growing up.

As a single mother, I went to P.T.A. meetings alone. I was their only parent who rooted for them when they participated in their sports activities, praised them when they succeeded, consoled them when they were upset, and disciplined them when they did something wrong. That was the hard part. It isn't fun to have to make unpopular decisions.

I remember the time when Peggy Ann was furious with me for grounding her for a month. "We'll never be friends!" she cried (as only a teenage soap opera fanatic can). I wanted to be lenient and cut the grounding period in half, but I stiffened and replied, "I have plenty of friends and I don't need you for a friend! You are my daughter!" She was

furious with me at the time, but today we are best friends.

I glanced down at Mike as he slept. Except for the mustache, he looked just like he did when he was a child. As I watched him sleep, I felt so thankful that I had been able to be home with all my children as they grew up.

I had never agreed with the idea that it was "quality time" that was important when raising children. I think it's quantity time that counts. A child can't be expected to concentrate all the important things he or she feels and thinks into some arbitrary hour or day that a parent designates as "quality time."

When Mike was two, he had interrupted my house cleaning 17 times in one hour! I'd counted them because I wanted to be able to justify to my husband why I could never get the whole house cleaned up. One of his interruptions was just to show me the inside of the dog's lips; unimportant by my standards, but a great discovery in his life. Another interruption was to inform me that he had accidently unplugged one of my house plants.

In the end, the person who is there all the time is the one who gives quality time. I was glad that I hadn't missed any part of my children's lives. They had grown up so fast! I had such wonderful times with them, but there had been some hard times, too.

I recalled the first time Mike didn't come home when he said he would. He was 16. He had driven to swing choir practice and had said he'd be home by 9:30 at the latest. I had gone to bed about 9 o'clock and had drifted into that fringe sleep where I could still hear. I had kept listening for the sound of the garage door going up. I must have been very tired, because the next time I looked at the clock, it was midnight. I raced to the laundry room and opened the door to the garage, and his car wasn't there! It was late, but I didn't care. I called Jackie Smith's house (Mike had taken him to practice.) His mom answered the phone (I woke her up) and told me that Mike had dropped Jackie off around 9:15.

I hung up and called the sheriff. He said that there hadn't been any accidents. He told me they couldn't file a missing person report until Mike had been gone for 24 hours. I told him that I thought that was a stupid rule. "When a person reports a missing person, the person is missing, and the person that reports it doesn't care if the person's been gone for ONE hour or 24!"

"I'm sorry but it doesn't work that way."

"OK. How 'bout if we say this, choir practice was LAST night.'"

He patronized me. "Now, Ma'am, I'm sure your son is all right and he'll have a logical explanation. You give me a call as soon as he comes in."

The sheriff calmed me down enough so that I could visualize the homecoming. "Yeah, you'll be hearing from me. As soon as he walks in the door, I'll kill him and call you back to report a homicide."

Time passed. I was frantic! Every siren I heard sent a shiver of fear through me, and then I'd feel guilty for being so negative. I waited until two in the morning and, when I couldn't stand it any longer, I got in my car, raised the garage door and backed into Mike's front bumper. It was the first time he had EVER left his car out all night.

I had to call the sheriff back and tell him that my son had been found. He asked me where he'd been, and I had to tell him that he'd been asleep in his bed and that I had failed to look out in the driveway for his car.

It's difficult bringing up children when two parents are actively involved. When one parent has the whole responsibility, it can be overwhelming. On one of our visits to "The 700 Club," my sister and I talked to the talent coordinator, Jackie Mitchum, who had reared a son by herself. She told us that there were times when she felt overburdened by the responsibility and, at one point during an exceptionally stressful time, she cried out, "Lord! I cannot be father and mother to this child." The Lord spoke to her heart and said, "I didn't call you to be the father and mother to this child. I called you to be his mother. I will be his father." From that point on, she said everything was much easier. Her son is now a very successful pastor.

I had always known that I wasn't alone when the kids were growing up. Whenever I was confused about what to do, or swallowed up by some problem, I knew that God was with me. That power has far more influence than the presence of any biological father.

I knew I could write volumes on my experiences as a single parent, but right now I needed to work on the article.

At 11:30 the guys woke up. The instant that the sleep was out of their eyes, I started on them to get the place cleaned up. I began with what I would describe as mild scolding, which promptly turned into moderate complaining. By the time I left to meet my sister for lunch, I was repulsed by the sound of my own voice, but at least my house looked like the kind of place where the author of a book on home organization just might live.

Chapter Two

How Come It's <u>My</u> Kitchen?

Eddie's Villa Del Weenie (our old lunch hangout) lost its charm when Eddie lost his mind. (Three years earlier, his wife, Torteena, had run off with another man...the technician who came in monthly to service an enormous bull Eddie had built to mechanically drag the salad bar around the restaurant.) With regrets, we moved our palates and our problems to Ron Det Vous.

It's not spelled correctly, but Ron owns it and, translated, we think he thought it meant Ron and You. In Hazel Dell, nobody's French, so it works, and besides the food is fabulous! Ron Det Vous used to be called the Outhouse Deli. The folks in Hazel Dell DID understand that name and nobody wanted to eat there. Ron bought the restaurant, kept the decor and named the place after himself.

The light fixtures were made out of real tin garbage cans hung upside down from the ceiling. Each table was topped with a collector's assortment of the caps from various beer bottles, sealed in a couple of inches of resin, and there were mirrors, framed with real toilet seats, reminding customers of Ron Det Vous' history.

It was always packed at Ron's, but we never minded the wait. As we stood in line for lunch, we were both preoccupied with our own domestic state of affairs.

"You're awful quiet."

"Awfully quiet."

"Well, pardone, grammar queen!"

"Oh, I'm sorry. I'm just tired, I guess. I think I've got jet lag."

"Sissy?"

"Yeah?"

"We stayed on the West Coast. I think you only get to lag when you change time zones."

"Well, then I've got trip lag and I didn't sleep very well, either. I had a Molly Dodd dream."

"A Molly Dodd dream?"

"Yeah, it went from one depressing, insignificant event to another. Nothing ever mattered, nothing ever meant anything, nothing ever happened and, when I woke up, I felt like I'd wasted the night.

"When I go out of town everything falls apart, and it

takes me two or three days to get things back under control. Stuff really piles up fast. You can't see the top of my dresser for all the mail and Danny's junk on it...and the laundry! While I was gone nobody did a thing....No, I take that back. Danny had each of the kids wash and dry a load, but do you think they folded any of it? Of course not! It's all in a pile on the couch.

"It's like they think some laundry fairy will come through in the night, fold their clothes and put them neatly back in their drawers! They don't even bring their laundry to where I sort it. I get so sick of having to drag everybody's dirty clothes from their rooms to the washer. I've lost my feist."

"Why do you do it?"

"Because if I didn't, it wouldn't get done."

"That's disgusting!"

"I know it is! And you know what else? This morning, Danny had the NERVE to criticize my sorting procedure!"

"Huh?"

"Yeah. He said I shouldn't put the dirty laundry in piles in the hall. That's where I have to sort the clothes."

"Well, it'd be a little hard to do it in a laundry room with a batch of eleven German shepherd puppies in there."

"Nine. Rosie's first litter was eleven."

"Oh."

"Where was I?"

"Dirty laundry---piles in the hall..."

"Oh, yeah. Danny's no laundry expert! He wouldn't need ANY place to make piles because he doesn't know you have to separate the colors! He'd throw 'em all in together, like the time I had the flu and he washed the pink throw rug with his black slacks and underwear. He even threw in his tie!"

Finally it was our turn at the cash register, where Ron's wife took our order. As usual, we split a hot pastrami supreme on dark rye, and each ordered a salad with ranch dressing.

"Sissy, do you think people who read our books, picture our houses just immaculate?"

"Sure, they do."

"That makes me feel bad."

"It really shouldn't. We've never claimed to be perfect. We've always admitted that we have a problem with organization. Besides, we were gone for three days. Why should we feel guilty for getting behind on the house, when we weren't even there?

"I hate the pressure of everything in the house falling on the woman's shoulders. Give me a break! It's not women's work inside and men's work outside! It's people-who-live-in-the-house work!"

"That's true, but a lot has to change in the male brain before it'll show up in the laundry room. Remember when we were at the vet and Dr. Slocum asked if we were working on a new project?"

"Yeah. I told him we were putting together a class to get husbands to do half and he said, 'Half of what?' When you said, 'Half of the household management, cooking and child care,' he looked at you like you'd told him he needed to buckhank and fleckhammer his vandecrod more often. Your words did not compute."

"Wasn't that interesting?"

"Yeah, but I'll bet those words would draw a blank with most men. 'Course there is that...what's his name...that preacher on television...he does everything!"

"I wish there was a way to keep the clutter under control without nagging. I get so frustrated with everybody. When five people each leave out a few things, the place looks a mess even if it's clean. I mean, who cares if the blinds are dusted and light fixtures shine, when there's junk everywhere you look?

"I'm just as guilty as the next guy. I left my makeup and stuff all over the bathroom counter and I haven't even unpacked yet!, but I feel like I'm responsible for everybody else too, and that's not fair.

"You should see the house right now! It's a cave because, ever since I got home, my energy's been on the McCall's article. I haven't had time to do the breakfast dishes so the kitchen's a mess; there's a huge pile of laundry to fold; we're out of groceries, and everybody's finger is pointed at me!"

"Well, I left my house clean, but everybody's MAD at me. Last night, before I went out with Terry, I threw a fit over Peggy's messes everywhere and she finally cleaned them up, but then Mike and his friends came over and made new ones. All I do is nag. I'm sick of the sound of my own voice."

We ate our lunch and talked about how we'd like things to be different.

"You know what I'd like? I'd like it if everybody just automatically cleaned up after himself, that's all! If they'd just take care of their own messes. Doesn't that make sense? If you trim your beard over the sink, clean up the whiskers before you leave the bathroom."

"Yeah, and if you take a bath, you clean the ring."

"And the last guy out of the bed makes it."

"Right! How about when you use the last square of toilet paper, you replace the roll?"

"Absolutely! Who buys the toilet paper?"

"The one with the most time, but the guy who shops doesn't have to haul the stuff from the car or put it away."

"That's fair. Who cooks?"

"I love to cook. But I shouldn't have to do the dishes."

"Of course not! Each eater should do his own dishes!"

"What about the pots and pans?"

"You don't touch them! If you cook the meal, they clean up after it!"

"Whoa, that would be interesting."

"What do you mean?"

"Think about it....They're used to being served and cleaned up after. They wouldn't like that."

"Well, it's only fair."

"I know that, but just because it's fair doesn't mean they'd like it. How would you like it if, all of a sudden, we came here and ate our lunch and then found out we had to bus our own dishes and help out in the kitchen before we could leave? You'd hate it! Ron would be out of business in less than a week!"

"I see what you mean. But here, we're paying for the service. At home it's all free."

"That makes me wild. My time is not free!"

"Maybe you should start charging for meals and kitchen work."

"Yeah, or maybe I oughta go on a strike like that lady in People Magazine did."

"What ever happened to her?"

"I don't know. Nothing, I guess."

"When I remarry, you can bet my husband will take care of himself! I won't be waiting on him hand and foot! He'll have to get up out of that recliner chair and do his half."

"Yeah, but he'll be used to it. He'll know what it takes to run a home because he's been on his own. Danny was 19 when we got married. He went from being taken care of by his mother to being waited on by me."

"You were a fool to get that started."

"Yeah, but I thought it was fun for awhile...and then we had the three kids all in three years 'cause you told me you can't get pregnant if you're nursing, and we got a bigger house and German shepherds and a cockatiel and two cats and I started a business....I don't know when, exactly, but waiting on everybody and picking up after them stopped being fun."

"What are you going to do?"

"I'm going to go home and throw a fit! I'll line the kids up and, through clenched teeth, I'll demand that they take an interest in having a clean house! I'll look Danny in the eye and tell him exactly what's wrong, and I'll insist things change! I'll tell him the days of Father Knows Best are over!"

"Schwooo...I love it!"

"I'll say, 'Look, Danny, while you're propped up in your easy chair reading the evening paper, I'm sweating over a hot stove!'"

"Oh, that's good."

"Yeah. I'll say, 'You expect me to wash your clothes and have them hanging in your closet, all starched and ironed, and what thanks do I get?...None!'"

"Yeah!"

"I'll say, 'Who balances the checkbook? Who picks up the boys from swimming practice and tennis classes? Who takes Ally to horseback riding lessons, and who takes the dogs to get their shots? Me! I mean, I!'"

"Ooo, yeah, watch your grammar."

"Yeah, I don't want him correcting me on anything! I'll say, 'Danny, the time has come for you to bond with the dogs!'"

"What'll he say?"

"He's a reasonable man. He'll see that things have to change. He's always real open and receptive to whatever I need. I'll just sit down with him and explain how I feel and everything'll be fine."

We finished our lunch and, grateful to stand up and distribute the weight of the pastrami, went to our office to proofread the article.

Even though we liked the ideas we had come up with, we knew they were, for the most part, Band-Aid tips that wouldn't do anything to change anyone's behavior permanently. The title, "Fifteen Hassle-Free Ways to Get Your Family to Help Around the House," bothered us. It implied manipulation, and we didn't want to have to GET anybody to help around the house; we wanted them to WANT to do their part.

The fact that our article was going to be published in a woman's magazine implied that it would be the woman who would be doing the manipulating; the mother would still be responsible for domestic order. Sports Illustrated would never think of featuring an article titled, "Fifteen Hassle-Free Ways to Get Your Family to Help Around the House." Why? Because most men don't feel that the house is their responsibility, and they would never read it.

We wished there was some way to cause the whole family to become aware and accountable for their share of the load, because we were trying to do it ALL, and we were being swamped by the backwash of people, places and things.

Chapter Three

Can This Marriage Be Saved?

I went back to my cave after Pam and I sent the article. I felt as if I needed a nap, partly because I was regrouping from the trip and partly because I felt stress over the house. *I'll start in the kitchen and get that under control.* I walked onto the porch, up and over the pile of dirt. *No, first I'll get the shovel and dig out the entry way and then I'll do the kitchen.* I went into the house. It could have been my imagination, but it even smelled messy. *I know a meal tastes better when it looks good. I wonder if it's the same kind of deal with a house. Maybe a home smells better when there's no clutter.*

"Hi...," I called to Jeff and Ally. "Did Chris call to be picked up?"

"Not yet, but Dad called! He said, 'Tell your mother,

thanks!'"

"What?"

"Yeah, I think you're in trouble."

"I'm in trouble...for what?"

"I don't know. Maybe you'd better call him."

"I will!"

"Hi, Mom," Ally chirped. Then her tone darkened. "Oh, did Dad get a hold of you? He's furious! He came home to change his clothes 'cause when he was in court and he crossed his legs, ya know?"

"Yeah?"

"His skin showed."

"And that's supposed to be MY fault? Your father needs new clothes...but he hates to go shopping! Is it my fault that he doesn't have much to choose from?"

"I don't know, Mom. I just know he's real mad."

"Yeah, well, I'm mad too!"

The look on Allyson's face made me feel guilty for dragging her into something that Danny and I should have settled privately.

"Never mind, Ally. I'll call Dad and we'll get this ironed out."

I jabbed out his number on my cordless and waited for the phone to ring. He answered.

"I understand you have a problem with me!" My enun-

69

ciation was crisp and cool.

"Yes, I do. Is it too much to ask to have clean clothes in the closet?"

"Yes! Right now it is. I think your timing stinks! You know I've been out of town and I've been working on a deadline. Things are a little behind."

"A little behind? The place is a pit! You've been home for three days and you still haven't unpacked. You haven't been to the store; the yard is a trash hole from the dogs running wild...I don't know what your problem is, but you sure seem to be spinning your wheels."

"You're right, Danny. You don't have a clue about what my problem is, because part of the problem is YOU!"

"Oh, sure. Blame YOUR disorganization on me! That's right. It's my fault! It's all MY fault!"

"I didn't say that. You're not listening!"

"Great, now I'm deaf! I'm tired of this conversation. The fact is, you really don't care. You let everything go until I can't stand it any more and I blow up. The kids are in their own little world, too. They know they're supposed to clean up after the dogs, but do they? You just try to walk across the lawn without slipping in one of the piles! Nobody cares. For days I've stepped over a styrofoam meat tray in the driveway, wondering how long it would stay there. If I didn't bend over and pick it up and put it in the garbage can myself, it'd be there until Ted Bundy gets the chair!"

"Danny, you say we're in our own little world, but you

don't realize what that means. We've all got pressures beyond the garbage in the driveway. You act like the kids and I are a bunch of no-good, lazy, shiftless slackers!"

(I dried the mouthpiece with my sleeve, took a deep breath and continued.) "You're oblivious to what we all do while you're at work. Give some credit where it's due! You've always said, 'Homework comes first!' and they're on the honor roll. So the piles on the lawn don't always get attention. Well, evidently they've learned to prioritize between dog poop and good grades!

"Chris works five days a week at the pizza place; he swims on the team and plays tennis, and he goes to Civil Air Patrol once a week. And Jeff, he works weekends mowing lawns, and answers the phone at our office, and he practices with the diving team five nights a week.

"Now Ally, she's not old enough to get a job yet, but she helps me with dinner every night and does anything I ever ask her to do! She's student body president; she plays the piano and takes horseback riding lessons in Battle Ground two days a week--and who do you think carts them all over the place? When I'm not chauffeuring them to all THOSE places, I'm hauling them to the orthodontist or somewhere else they have to be, or I'm in the office working, or Pam and I are writing...or I'm here at home trying to keep things up! If we missed the meat tray, we are sorry! But we are NOT a bunch of bums!"

"I didn't say you were bums. I'm only pointing out that the house is filthy."

71

"No, it isn't! It's very clean and you know it! It's just a little messy."

"Ok, it's messy then. Call it what you want, but there isn't one room that looks clean. That's the way it goes. You let it keep getting worse until I explode, then you run around cleaning things up, and for awhile you have the house in order, but then you get sidetracked and things are right back where they were."

"Excuse me? I get sidetracked? I get sidetracked because there are too many tracks, and I can't be on all of them at once! You think you're the only one who wants a clean house? Right now it's probably bothering me more than it's bothering you! I just have a longer fuse and more tolerance...and I DON'T blame you for the circumstances that have led to the mess. That's where we're different! You hold ME responsible. Well, it's too much! I can't do it all any more!"

"Then figure it out and cut back."

"Cut back on what? The laundry maybe? I think that's how this whole argument got started. What would you have me cut back on?"

"That's for you to figure out. I don't know your schedule. Just quit playing games and take care of it."

"Playing games...that's wonderful!"

"You are. It's the poor-me game. Get serious and figure out some kind of a work schedule and then stick to it."

"FINE!" I swallowed back the tears. My throat hurt so

much that the ache went deep into my chest as I mustered my last stand. "Danny, one more thing. The next time you have a grievance with me, DON'T deliver it through the children. It's certainly not fair to them, and it shows absolutely no respect for my position!"

I was proud of the way I had stood up for myself in spite of the lump in my throat. I had spoken as articulately as William Buckley.

It was quiet.

"Yes...I'm sorry about that. I was wrong."

I couldn't talk. The lump had my voice box in a squeeze.

"I'll see you tonight." His tone softened.

"Yeah." I slammed the AT&T into its cradle and let the tears burst.

How could he be so insensitive about my feelings? "Quit playing the poor-me game!" Ha! How could he put so little value on my efforts and my time? Why didn't he recognize my contribution and see that I'm not able to take care of the house and his needs the way I did before I started my business? He was acting like he thinks I don't care. Does he really believe that, or was it just a cheap shot? All HE seems to care about is 'how does this affect me?' It affects him because I'm not there to cater to him, feed him and wash his clothes! I don't expect HIM to wait on ME. I'd never think to call to him from the shower to see if he bought shampoo. I wouldn't dream of asking him to lay out an outfit for me to wear to a speech.

He knows the subject of organization is a touchy one with

me, and how dare he throw the word "sidetracked" in my face? He knows that's the theme of one of my books! "Figure out a work schedule and stick to it!" Yeah, but don't figure him into it! I should have said, "How dare you even suggest that this is MY problem!" I should have told him to mind his own business! No, that's a cliche. I should have said, "Until you are ready to be reasonable, there is no point in discussing this any further."

Yeah, I should have used words like "perhaps" and "occasionally."

"Perhaps I am occasionally dilatory in my responsibilities, both to my business and my home. However, I am endeavoring to maintain a balance between the two and keep my mental, emotional and physical vehicles intact."

No, he'd say, "Stop playing the pseudo-intellectual game." I can't believe he was so hateful. How could he attack me as a homemaker? He knows my family is the most important thing in my life. He just doesn't understand. That's all. "Figure it out and cut back!" Ha! I oughta keep a time log of everything I do! Would he ever have his eyes opened!

I got a spurt of energy at the thought of making a list of my work load compared to his. I would make that list and, at the next confrontation, I'd be ready! Meanwhile, I'd get the kids to help me straighten up the house.

In less than half an hour, the place looked terrific, proving my point that it was purely superficial clutter and not filth.

When Danny came home that night, we were coolly cordial. Polite, yet barely looking at each other, neither of us cared to take up where our phone conversation had left off. Both of us were overly pleasant to the children and obviously indifferent to each other. I was still fighting off hurt feelings and waves of tears. At the dinner table I said I wasn't very hungry and excused myself. Sneaking a chicken leg from the platter in the kitchen, I took a paper towel, went to the bedroom and ate the poultry in the dark.

It was only eight o'clock, but I was exhausted. The fight had worn me out. I positioned myself as far over on my side of the bed as I possibly could without dropping off the edge. I was determined to cling there all night. "Ha!" I muttered to myself. "Cut back! I can think of ONE thing I'll be cutting back on, starting tonight!" I slept, but never so deeply as to risk drifting closer to the enemy. Danny kept on his edge, too.

In the morning, I got up without speaking. When I looked in the bathroom mirror, I scared myself. I noticed my cheek had what looked like a large, serious scar across it. (It was just an indentation from the cording on the edge of the mattress.) My eyes were puffy and bloodshot from crying myself to sleep, and there was a little bit of barbecue sauce from the chicken, left on my chin.

I went into the kitchen to make coffee and noticed it was immaculate! *I'll bet the kids did the dishes for me. They'd do anything right now to ease the tension around here.*

"Are you and Dad still mad at each other?" Chris asked. He looked worried. Danny and I rarely argue, and our real fights are limited to about two a year: one in the spring when

we take the boat out for the first trip of the season, and the other in the fall when we decide whether or not to sell it.

"Yeah, Chris, we're still mad, but we'll work it out. I could use your help, though. Dad seems to feel like no one cares about the house and the yard the way he does. I don't think that's true. I think we do care, but we're all so busy and we're going in so many different directions that it's hard to keep on top of everything."

"Yeah, I know."

"I'm going to talk to Jeff and Ally and get them to be more aware of picking up their things and helping with the laundry and dishes, but it's going to take all of us."

"Dad too?"

"Yeah, Dad too. But for right now, I think we should be concerned about our own habits."

"Okay." We hugged each other.

"Start this morning by sorting your laundry."

"Where should I put it, in the hall?"

"Uh...no. I'll set up a place in the laundry room. The puppies are getting too big to be in there. It's time for them to go outside."

Ally came into the kitchen with a little cloud of concern over her head. "Are you and Dad fighting?"

"Hmm...I think we already fought. Now we're thinking about what we said to each other, and probably for awhile we're both going to be upset."

77

"How come?"

"Because we agree there's a problem, but neither of us knows what to do about it yet. One thing I can tell you for sure....I love your dad and he loves me. On a scale of one to ten, if one would be a dirty look and ten would be a divorce, this fight would only be about a five." (She didn't need to know that, during our phone fight, we were hovering around 15!) "You don't need to worry, but it would help if you would be extra careful to see that the house stays neat." She agreed.

Next Jeff confronted me. "How come Dad was so mad yesterday?" he pried.

"Because he looked bad and he didn't know who to blame. His hair didn't work because we were out of shampoo; he needs new clothes...I don't know...the house was a mess. I've been gone and he's had to be both mother and father...I think everything just came to a head at once and we both exploded."

"What do you need me to do?"

"Just make sure that you take care of your own messes. That alone will make a big difference."

"I will."

I easily had the support and cooperation of all three of the children. I praised them and acknowledged what each was already doing to help. Then we talked about what they could do to make things better around the house and easier for their father and me. I had to wonder why I wasn't able to talk to Danny in the same comfortable way I could talk to the children. Our conversation had been accusatory and hostile. Maybe it was because our egos were involved, but all we had succeeded in doing was to create bad feelings.

$\mathcal{L}ess$ $\mathcal{T}han$ $\mathcal{F}riendly$ $\mathcal{P}ersuasion$

When I left our office (we'd had to Federal Express the article to meet the deadline), I thought about the fight Peggy was going to have. Getting cooperation from her unsuspecting spouse of 20 years could be tricky. I was glad I didn't have to deal with that problem. Being single for ten years, I had promised myself that any man I became interested in would have to know, or at least be willing to learn, basic homemaking skills, before I would ever consider marriage.

It was true that most of the men I'd encountered were pathetic in that area. (Peggy and I had considered teaching a beginner's homemaking class for men only, after I'd gone through a string of retarded male homemakers. We agreed, however, that no man would come to a class like that unless we held it in a tavern, served beer and pretzels and had wide-screen sports at the breaks.)

Terry was the new man in my life, and he was certainly no exception to the domestic retardation I'd seen in my previous dates. I liked him a lot and was seriously working on improving his skill level, because I could see his potential.

I had invited him over for dinner and, since it would be his first meal in my home, I had decided to be extra careful that the evening's work load would be equal. I even called him at his office and told him we would be going to the supermarket together before we made dinner. He was pleased with the pronoun, "we," and he agreed to take off a little early to allow time for the shopping.

We had fun together at the store, though I felt a bit as if I were taking a kindergartner on a field trip. Here was a 44-year-old man, who had been single for two years and was feeding primarily on canned soup and peanut butter sandwiches.

In the grocery store, the produce section was as foreign to him as the underside of a car would be to me. He soaked up every bit of information I gave out as we passed the colorful variety of fruits and vegetables. He was pleased to know that he could buy just one or two potatoes instead of a ten-pound sack. When we came to the bananas, I chose a nice yellow bunch and tore it in half, putting three in the cart. He had a look on his face as if he'd just witnessed a bank hold-up.

"You can do that!?" he whispered, as he wielded a guilty glance around the produce department to see if anyone had seen me.

"You mean rip a bunch of bananas apart?"

"Yeah...that's really okay to do?" He was still nervous, as if he'd been an accomplice in a crime.

"Of course, it's okay to do that. What did you think would happen: sirens, loud speakers: 'Guy in produce, rippin' off bananas!'?"

He liked what I had told him and stripped off one more banana to test the validity of what he had learned. No sirens...no loud speakers...no irate produce manager....It really WAS okay!

With the bananas behind us, I asked him to get some carrots, celery, lettuce and a couple of pounds of broccoli, while I finished getting the fruit. He took the shopping cart and headed for the greens.

When I was finished with my selections, I joined him. He looked anxious for my approval as he cocked his head sideways, motioning me to check the cart. "I got everything you told me to," he beamed.

I beamed back and turned to put my fruit with his vegetables. I was mortified to see what he had done! He had torn a head of romaine lettuce in half, severed four stalks of celery from the rest of their family and decapitated all the broccoli florets from their stems, leaving the heavy stalks next to the scale. It was so unbelievable that my mouth started moving before my ability to edit what was coming

SNAP!

out could take over. A flurry of superlatives hit Terry in the face.

When my social-awareness alarm caught up with my tongue, I was embarrassed, and Terry looked like a dog that didn't know why he was in trouble. He needed more hands-on training...but not in public. I wondered if I could get him a video on grocery store etiquette that he could view in the privacy of his own home.

Leaving the spoils behind, I reluctantly rolled him into the meat department. I rang the bell for the butcher.

"What does that do?"

I hate sarcasm, but I couldn't resist. "It rings the butcher, who lives in the back with all his little barnyard friends. When he hears the bell, he'll come out and we'll tell him that we want this chicken sawed in half."

"In half, why?" he winced.

"Well, because we are going to barbecue it. After it's in half, we'll take it home and put the halves on the grill. Then the meat will cook from the inside out." I was beginning to feel the superiority of my vast culinary knowledge.

The butcher appeared, looking as though he'd been on the front lines. I was amused that he knew I was the one who had interrupted his work, even though Terry had the chicken in his hand. "What can I do ya for, ma'am?"

Terry held the chicken out as if he were holding a dead possum he'd found on the freeway, and gestured, with a slicing motion, to cut the bird in half. "We'd like this cut in two pieces, please." His voice was definite and authoritative.

"Ha! You want it cut that way?" (Terry's cutting motion had divided the hen's top from its bottom.) "Which one of you guys is gonna get the butt and the two legs?" The butcher laughed. "I'm a breast man, myself! How 'bout you?"

Terry laughed, too.

I interrupted their sexist fun over the chicken parts, took the package out of Terry's hand and instructed, "Just cut it right, please."

We were in the store much too long.

At home, I had Terry light the charcoal. (I made a mental note of the time it took.) When he was through watching the flames and was sure the briquettes were going to burn, he went out to the street to get the newspaper.

I let him sit down long enough to get comfortable. "Terry!" I called from the kitchen.

"What?" He sounded as if he were responding to a lilting request.

"Will you please make the salad?"

It was interesting to find out that his idea of a salad was chopped lettuce. I was stunned to discover that his idea of salad dressing was mayonnaise. Not even mayo and catsup; just mayonnaise. I enlightened him. We made Caesar salad together.

I saw to it that the meal preparations were absolutely

equal. By the time we were ready to eat, I was hoarse from the cooking lesson and he was much more aware of what goes into fixing a good dinner. The paper was never read, but we set the table together and took turns basting the chicken. Terry snipped half the beans and learned how to clarify butter. I cut up my half of the strawberries and, while he sliced his, I showed him how to make the roux. We shared in the preliminary clean-up and, when we sat down to eat, he was exhausted and had almost lost his appetite.

After the meal, he was ready to throw himself back on the couch and relax. That's when the flare-up occurred....There were still dishes to do.

The next morning, I called my sister.

"I think a class to get men to do half is a generation away. Terry left last night with the look of a freed slave, and I don't think he'll call for a while, either; at least not until he recuperates from the big dinner! You know what? I hate being demanding. I get help with the housework only because I resort to screaming and nagging. The kids oblige, but it's always a big fight. And now Terry...I'm sure I'm listed in his little black book under 'B' instead of 'Y.'

"The darned thing about that is I love to cook, and I would've rather done it myself. It's relaxing to me. I feel creative. I love the appreciation for a fabulous meal...but I was afraid if I let him sit there and read the paper, he'd get the idea that HIS place was in the LA-Z-BOY! Isn't THAT interesting? They don't make a LA-Z-GIRL recliner!"

"Oh, brother!"

"I don't want to end up with a man who's unwilling to do his share. Maybe I was wrong to insist we do everything together. It would have been all right if I had cooked alone, as long as he helped with the cleanup. I hate to do the dishes after I've cooked. But who doesn't? I mean, do you know anyone who finds 'cleanup' fulfilling? I'll bet the Women's Liberation Movement was started by a bunch of homemakers who got sick and tired of cleaning up after everybody.

"I hope I didn't scare Terry away with my equal rights crusade. Do you think he'll call me? ....Hello? ...Sissy, are you in there?"

"No, I'm not! Here I've been in love with a man for two decades, and I find out his devotion is only as deep as a pile of dirty laundry! You're asking me if I think Terry will call you? Quite frankly, Charlotte, I don't give a rip!"

"Well!"

"Oh, I'm sorry, Sissy....I'm just upset. Danny and I had a huge fight last night."

"Ohhhh...right, I forgot about you guys! Did you win?"

"No. But neither did he. We're at a stalemate. We're speaking, but there is definitely a chill in the air!"

"What are you going to do?"

"I don't know yet. We'll have to talk it out sooner or later. I'm not looking forward to it. Have you ever had to argue with a policeman?"

"No."

"It's a losing deal! Danny puffs up and his lips disappear."

"I think all men do that when they're mad."

"Well, it's very intimidating."

"I know it!"

"I'm not going to get into any arguments until I have all my facts. I'm going to keep a log to show just exactly how I spend my day, compared to his. He may put in three or four more hours at his office than I do, but when he comes home, that's it! It's rest and relaxation. I come home in time to chauffeur the kids all over town, make dinner, clean up, do some laundry and then it's bedtime!"

"Oh, Sissy, it'll be so obvious that you do 'way more than he does."

"Yeah. But you know, Danny is a hard worker. I don't mean to sound like he doesn't do anything, because that's not true. He has totally remodeled the house, and his flower beds are impeccable. What gets me is that he leaves all the little day-in and day-out responsibilities to me. It's the things that SEEM insignificant, but collectively keep everything working, that he takes for granted. He doesn't notice until one of those 'little' things doesn't get done, and THEN it gets his attention. Maybe he'd be more appreciative if he was responsible for some of those little things himself.

"Before I confront him, I'm going to have a list of changes to negotiate."

"Like what?"

"Like I don't want to make his sack lunch any more. On the weekends, I don't want to make breakfast both mornings. I want him to make it on Saturday and I'll do it on Sunday. I don't want to make the bed after he gets out of it, and I want him to clean his own tub ring and wash his whiskers out of the sink.

"I think we should take turns taking and picking up the kids. I want him to do his own dishes and supervise the kitchen clean-up while I relax from cooking the meal. I want him to share the laundry responsibility, take turns going to the cleaners...and I don't EVER want to wrestle the German shepards, trying to get them to the vet again. They're just too big!

"I'm going to have all of this in writing. It's going to be in black and white so there's no misunderstanding."

"Do you think you'll cry?"

"Yes."

"Darn. Men hate tears!"

"I know, but I'm not going to worry about it. In fact, I'm going to plan the talk so that I can cry hard if I feel like it."

"Whoa!"

"Yeah, but I don't cry very often, so if I need to cry over this, I get to. It'd be different if I was sloppin' all over the house in tears every day. THESE tears will mean something."

"Good luck!"

We hung up and I sat at my desk, so grateful that I was single. I had to admit that in my middle years, I had become very cynical about men. My son, Mike, had recently warned me that I had more of a chance of being sniped by a terrorist than I had of ever remarrying! (Peggy told me I should start dating terrorists.) Quite frankly, I was in no hurry to do ANY knot-tying! I thought about Terry. *Wouldn't it be great if, when you got married, the guy came with a written guarantee stating that, if he didn't work out, you could take him back and get a new one?* The thought of it made me laugh and prompted me to specify my spousal requirements in a poem.

Warranty Man

You can bet that my next husband
Will come with a warranty.

Thirty years on parts and service,
He'll be trouble-free.

I will read that operator's manual

To figure our how he'll work.

I'll find out how to turn him on
And disconnect him when he's being a jerk.

I won't have to jump-start
His worn-out battery,

And if he starts to smoke,
He's going back to the factory.

I'll take all the extras,
As far as options go.

He's gotta have a nice size trunk
And be equipped with booze control.

I'll take him in for tune-ups;
They'll check his plugs and points.

They'll test his shock absorbers
And grease up his ball joints.

And when his road of life has ended,
I'll tow him faithfully,

Back to where he came from,
With a money-back guarantee.

93

Chapter Five:

Infraction's the Name of the Game

My warfare with Danny was far from over. Underneath the dirty laundry, there were deeply rooted male/female issues that needed to be weeded out and done away with forever.

I'm not sure when women got stuck with total responsibility for the home. I have my own theory that it goes back more than six million years. I think that in the beginning there was equality; male and female in perfect symmetry. Harmonious, even and well-balanced, the two were distinct without difference. Like two pieces in a jigsaw puzzle, opposite yet perfectly matched, the equivalents were complete...and then came mealtime. The dialogue went something like this:

"Great night's sleep! I'm hungry, are you?"

"Yeah, I guess so. My stomach feels kinda funny. Maybe I just need to eat."

"Do you want me to go out and get something while you keep the fire going?"

"It doesn't matter. I could go."

"Nah, your stomach's acting up. I'll go."

"Okay, you go get it and I'll cook it when you get back."

"Sounds fair to me."

"Good. I'll clean up around the cave and set the table."

"Great!"

One of them left in search of food, and the other stayed home and kept the cave warm. Outside, there were all kinds of scary beasts and giant flying reptilia, and food wasn't that easy to find. Meanwhile, back at the cave, the fire started to smoke, the queasy stomach got worse, and cave-to-cave solicitors kept the pregnant entity from getting a nap. Returning exhausted, the guy with the food was annoyed. He felt that the one who'd stayed behind didn't appreciate all he'd been through out in the world. The one in charge of the home fires also felt aggravated. The cave was boring and smoky; the partner was later than he'd said he'd be; the food didn't satisfy the craving, and the firewood was almost gone.

"How was your day?"

"Oh, just terrific. It's one big party out there."

"Yeah? Well, it wasn't that great being stuck here all

day, either!"

Day in and day out, the couple woke up, got the food, cleaned the cave, cooked, ate, argued and turned in for the night. Soon they were blessed with a child. The birth thrilled the co-creators, but with the added mouth to feed, the designated food-finder felt pressured to bring back even more. He began to leave earlier and stay out longer in search of provisions. After a tough day, he would often stop at a popular watering hole to enjoy the company of his fellow huntsmen. Commiserating over losses or swapping tales of brave victories, he'd usually lose track of time. Staggering home, dragging the catch of the day behind him, he would be greeted by his less than festive spouse.

While the father was out foraging, the mother nurtured the little cavette, teaching her right from wrong and the art of homemaking. The child tore around the cave, making messes, noise and trouble. Every year there was another child. When it became clear what was causing the pregnancies, the stretch-marked female and the hairy-chested Homo sapien had to cut back on their only form of entertainment (except for an occasional game of Pictionary).

When the cave got too crowded, the mother said to the father, "Take your sons with you today. The girls and I will clean the cave." Before anyone realized it, the roles were established....The male went out into the world and the female kept the home fires burning, and it didn't start changing until "Family Ties" and "The Cosby Show" were in the top ten.

Thursday, March 26, was a beautiful, fresh, sunny spring morning, except at the Joneses'. I was gray. I hated the way I felt. I was bitter and hurt, fragile and confused. I wanted to get out of the house. I borrowed Chris's Walkman, plugged myself into something classical (leaving Def Leopard on Chris's desk), and Rosie and I went for a walk. She needed to get away, too.

I live on the edge of a canyon, overlooking a lake and wildlife refuge. There is a paved path around the lake that winds through maple and evergreen trees and peacefully leaves the world behind. It's a perfect place to listen for answers to prayer. (I know you didn't buy this book in a religious bookstore, and the last thing you want to hear is a sermon, but if I don't say that I prayed for an answer to the problems I was having at home, there will be a hole in the telling of what happened to make things right.)

I let Rosie off her leash, and she ran ahead to drink and flounce around in the creek. Then I sat down on a big rock and I prayed.

"I don't know what to do, God. These feelings of bitterness and anger are choking me. I feel heavy and dark in my spirit. I can't see any light in this situation. I can't even look at Danny without getting mad! I've gone over and over the phone fight, and his words are more piercing every time. I need peace and a simple answer. I want us to understand each other. Please help me, God."

"Hey, you! Is that your German shepard?"

"Huh?" I opened my eyes and saw Rosie in the distance. She had treed a jogger! I ran to rescue the terrified man. "Rosie! Heel! Heel! Rose, heel! She won't hurt you; she's just smelling you! Rosie! Bad dog!" The man was frozen and speechless. "There, see, she's back on her leash. You can get down now. I'm so sorry she scared you! Are you all right?"

"If you ever walk this trail with that animal off his leash again, I'll call the cops so fast you won't have a prayer!"

I felt like Jimmy Stewart did after he'd prayed on Christmas Eve in "It's a Wonderful Life".

The dog and I walked back home and, although my heart was even heavier, the exercise and fresh air had felt good. The only answer I had seemed to hear was one word: "Rest." I hadn't slept well since the fight. He was right; I needed a nap.

Later that day, I was on my way to the store, still preoccupied with thoughts of my 48-hour domestic battle. The kids were being extra careful to see that their things were put away, but I knew it would only last as long as the cold war Danny and I were waging. Once the smoke cleared, things would pile up again, and I'd go right back to nagging and policing.

Just as I was thinking that it was a shame nobody was accountable without a fight, I noticed an abandoned car alongside the freeway. The highway patrol had tagged it. (Danny told me once that they tag cars before they tow them. The bright ticket is a signal to other circling troopers that the vehicle has been checked out, written up and earmarked for the hook. I think he said the owner has something like 24 hours to retrieve the lemon before Speedy's Tow Masters get it.)

I wondered what it would cost the guy. *Hmm...Too bad we don't have some kind of house patrol. Stuff left out would get tagged, and the owner would have just so much time to retrieve it without paying. Not a bad idea...make it official just like the state patrol does. Make the rules and enforce them.* I got excited. There was the simple answer I had asked for in my prayer.

While I was in the store, I bought a package of bright, fluorescent adhesive dots the size of a nickel. When I got home, I couldn't wait! I went through the house and put a dot on anything I found that had been left out. I was delighted that, since the children and I had made tidiness our life's work for the last couple of days, most of the tags appeared on Danny's things! I loved it! His tennis bag was in the entry hall, his shoes were under the coffee table, the newspaper was on the couch, his coffee mug was on the bathroom counter, his sunglasses were on top of the dresser, his Thermos was by the sink, and his sport coat was hung on the back of the kitchen chair. With pleasure, I tagged him in every room. The children watched me.

"What are you doing with those stickers, Mom? Are we going to have another garage sale?" Jeff was puzzled. "How come Dad's selling his good coat?"

"He's not. I'm just tagging it for being on the chair." As I made my final rounds, my inquisitive kids followed me.

"See all these things your father left out?"

"Yeah."

"I have decided to play a little game with him. You can play it, too. The main rule is, if it's not decorative, it shouldn't be out. If it's out, I will consider it abandoned and tag it as an infraction!"

"What's an infraction?" Ally asked.

"You know, it's like a...a violation."

"What about your stuff?"

"Huh?"

"Won't Dad tag you for your stuff?"

"Uh...sure, that's only fair. However, as you can see, all of my stuff is put away." There was arrogance in my tone.

"Mom?"

"Yes, Chris."

"I don't think your purse is a very good decoration on the piano."

"Well, no, but it's my purse and I need to be able to leave it out. You understand."

"Not really. If the main rule is that junk left out has to be a decoration or be put away, I think you'd better find another place for your purse or you'll get tagged for it." (I put my purse in the hall closet on the shelf. It was the last time I would ever have to look for it again!)

The kids and I talked about the new game in more detail,

making up the rules as we thought of them. Infractions would be counted for laundry and dishes left in bedrooms or any place else (one infraction per item), beds unmade, lights left on when the room is empty, tub rings, toilet seats left up, and coats, purses, books and anything else left out that shouldn't have been.

Since I had more time in the morning than anyone else, I said I'd empty the dishwasher first thing, so they could put their breakfast dishes in there. If they left them in the sink when the dishwasher was empty, they would be counted as infractions. The owner would have a reasonable amount of time to retrieve his or her belongings without penalty. We would write the time on the dot so there would be no arguments about how long items had been left out.

When the time limit expired, the infractions and the amount charged would be written on 3x5 cards (one for each person in the family) and would be posted on the bulletin board in the kitchen. We decided that 25 cents was a fair amount to charge for each item and agreed that, for one week, we would be on probation, adding up the money but not actually collecting it. It would give us a chance to be aware of how much our actions would cost us, once the game really started.

Then we discussed what we should do with the money. I thought it should go toward something decorative for the house (with all our junk put away, I could see the need for some tasteful knickknacks.)

"What's the object?" Chris asked.

"To have the house neat," I said.

"I think the object oughta be to win the money by having the fewest infractions. The clean house would just be a by-product," Jeff proposed.

I wasn't sure I liked the logic of my brilliant offspring. I wished that he cared more about a clean house and less about the money, but the other kids loved his idea.

We decided that we could all act as watchmen and tag each other. We called the game, Infraction! (I opted not to explain this new idea to Danny for awhile. Wicked as it may have been, I wanted to infract him as many times as I could. It would be evidence of his contribution to the mess and I would have it in black and white...and fluorescent red.)

During the next two days, we filled our 3x5 infraction cards with violations. (In one week, there would have been $19.75 in our kitty if we had actually collected the money.) The first day, Allyson had eleven bathroom infractions alone. After that, she rarely left anything out that we could tag. Chris had trouble leaving ice cream bowls in his room, and Jeff couldn't seem to get his backpack out of the hall each day after school. I was repeatedly tagged on my car keys, which soon joined my purse in the closet, and I also got penalized for leaving my watch on the windowsill (My watch is pretty, but they ruled that it was personally decorative rather than publicly decorative.)

Unbeknown to him, Danny was racking up the most violations. He was guilty of whiskers and tub rings, toilet seats, damp towels, dishes, mugs, mail and more. Since he was such a substantial contributor to the pot, we all looked forward to the day he'd find out he was a player and have to cough up the cash. I was second in line for the clutter crown; Jeff and Chris were tied for third (and eventually formed a union whereby they agreed not to infract each other and split the money, should they ever win it) and, after the first day, Allyson was the neatest.

For the short time that the kids and I had been on the new system, the house had never looked so consistently free of our clutter. The impact of something so simple was shocking. It had been so easy to enforce, yet its power was incredible. I wished that we hadn't created it out of desperation, but instead had run into it happily, in some "how to" book, without having to go through the fire.

Danny was still in the dark about the dots. I'd seen him pick one of the colored tattlers off of the seat of his pants (which had been carelessly tossed over a chair), and I thought to myself that he must surely be puzzled by its conspicuous grip on his backside. He had no idea what the little fluorescent dot meant or how much it would cost him in the future. I loved it!

It was Saturday morning, and Pam and I were supposed to give a luncheon speech on "Home Is Where The Heart Is." My heart wasn't in it. When a couple doesn't usually fight, a blow-up like the one Danny and I had had was especially debilitating. We both wanted a truce.

"We need to talk," Danny finally said. (Since I had suffered the most injustice, I felt that it was appropriate that he made the first advance toward peace.)

"Yes, I know we do, but when we talk, we need to have time to get everything that's bothering us out in the open. I know I'm going to cry hard, and I need to be able to do that without worrying about wrecking my make-up."

"All right."

"If it's okay with you, I'd like to postpone the talk until after my speech."

"That's fine. When will you be home?"

"About two."

"I'll be here."

I had had time to think and so had he. We were both prepared for the confrontation. At two o'clock we met in our bedroom, closed the door, sat on the bed and faced each other. (I was glad that I was dressed up and looked my best. He didn't look that good.) It's hard to argue with a policeman, but it's probably just as difficult to have a talk with someone who earns her living giving speeches and writing books. The "talk" took two hours.

"I'm sorry for the things I've been thinking about you," I confessed.

"So what's going on?"

"I've given it a lot of thought and I've really prayed about it, because I want to understand both sides. I think there are several things happening to us right now."

"Like what?"

"I feel like you take me for granted. It doesn't seem like you appreciate all the things I do for you and the family. You're quick to point out what I haven't done and slow to notice what I have."

"So are you."

"What? In what way?" (It was news to me!)

"Last Saturday, for instance, I spent all day in the yard while you were shopping, and you came home and didn't even notice."

"I did, too! I told you it looked real nice."

"Yeah, well, maybe I would have felt like you really meant it if you'd taken a minute to walk around and really look at it."

"You're right. I should have, and I was going to come back out as soon as I took my packages in, but then I got busy and forgot. I'm sorry. I guess we both do that. The other day I was so proud of myself for hemming your new jeans right away and I said, 'Guess what, Danny? Your new jeans are hemmed and ready to wear!' and you said, 'Good. Did you sew up the pocket in my jacket?' I needed 'way more points for that!"

"I'm sorry. I'll try to be more appreciative."

"So will I."

"So what else?" He took out his pipe and started his tamping ritual (a sign that he was vulnerable and needed the motions to give him time to think).

"I want you to lighten up."

He stared at me.

"You're always finding what's wrong." (I countered his tamping with some nail filing.) "Like Saturday, after you and the boys worked so hard all day in the yard, you stood back and looked at what you'd done and Chris said, 'It sure looks good, huh, Dad?' and you said, 'Yeah, but it needs barkdust.' I saw Chris and Jeff just look at each other."

"Really? Well, I didn't mean that I didn't appreciate how much they did. I could just see what else we still had to do."

"You do it a lot. Someone will say, 'Dad, the pool sure looks great!' and you'll say, 'Yeah, but we need to scrub the tiles!' If you could just stop yourself before you say, 'Yeah, but...'"

"I don't mean to do that. It's just that there's always something that needs to be done."

"I know, and that's the point. When you say, 'We can't play until the work is done,' you forget that the work is NEVER done! So where's the time for fun?"

"Hmm..."

"I watched you last summer with the pool. You scrubbed it, vacuumed it, chlorinated it, back-washed it and tested it constantly, but did you ever swim?"

"Not very much."

108

"You need to kick back and play more."

"Sometimes it irritates ME that you can play no matter what needs to be done. Remember when the McLains called and asked us to go on a picnic to Lewisville Park? You were right in the middle of wallpapering the little bathroom, but you said, 'Sure! We'd love to go!' I couldn't believe it! I wish you would take things a little more seriously."

"We're so different from each other, aren't we?"

"Yep. That's probably why, after twenty years, we're still intrigued with each other."

We were making progress, but there was still the issue of work loads to be discussed. I had abandoned the idea of throwing a time log in Danny's face because I decided I didn't have to prove my value that way, to him or anyone else!

Initially I had divided a piece of notebook paper in half lengthwise, with his name at the top of one side and mine at the top of the other, but, staring at the blank college rule, I changed my mind. I wasn't afraid to align my day with his, hour by hour; I just hated the nit-picky thought of, *Okay, let's see, it's 6:15. I'm making the coffee and what is HE doing? Ah ha! Still in bed, I see. Log it!*

I also hated it because of the ramifications of the hourly comparison. I could just hear what he'd be thinking: *Hmm...it's 12:45 and I don't have the time to stop and eat! I wonder what SHE is doing. I think I'll call her at the office.*

"Hi, is Peggy there?...She's at the Ron Det Vous?...When did she leave?...11:30? (Very interesting!) Would you have her

*call me when her lunch hour and a half is over?" I'll log in
exactly how many minutes she spent eating!*

Danny has no idea of how often I take a long, late lunch,
spoiling my appetite and allowing me to give the impression
at dinner that I eat like a bird. Depending on which day was
being logged, the work load scale could tip in my favor or
not. Some days, Danny works overtime or goes out of town,
and he doesn't get home again until the next day or even the
next week. That is the nature of his job. Other days, I'm the
one who has to work late or travel. It would be very difficult
to determine who is working the hardest, because we both
work hard.

Apart from each other, we live completely different
lives. He deals with all the ugliness in the world, and I'm a
humorist. We couldn't be more opposite. If we were totally
honest with each other, we would admit that neither of us
really knows what the other's day is like. We do know that
we wouldn't trade places with each other for anything!

Danny can't imagine how I can get up in front of a
thousand people and give a speech, or go on television and
not faint. He says it would scare him more than raiding an
outlaw biker's party. (One time when he had to give the
crime report on the local radio station, he said it was 90
seconds of Hell! Unable to think of the word deceased, he
said, "We are investigating the identity of the...ah...dead
fellow." He was embarrassed!)

On the other hand, if I had to do the things Danny has
had to do, like wade through the filth of a drug dealer's

house, wrestle a vomiting drunk into my car, hold a dying man's head, break up a fight between a man and his wife, rescue a baby from a burning house, shoot a bank robber, go to an autopsy or investigate a murder...I couldn't do it!

One thing we do have in common, we both know the feeling of working our faces off, with no rewards or applause. I have seen Danny's frustration at the end of a day, when he has nothing to show for all of his efforts. He can work a case for months, finally arrest the crook, do all the paperwork and, on his way home, pass the guy on the freeway because he's been released on bail or the jails are too crowded. Like homemaking, police work can be a thankless, losing battle.

I was sure that Danny admired my work from a distance, the same as I respected what he was doing. Still, I didn't think he would appreciate all the time I spent visiting with my sister. On a time log, it wouldn't look that good. I was afraid Danny wouldn't recognize the value of those "visits," even though they inevitably earned us a substantial amount of money. When we were together, we came up with our most profound thoughts, humorous viewpoints and creative ideas, which turned into books, speeches and television appearances.

Granted, some of our ideas didn't pan, like a new line of fragrances we were toying with, called "Smells Like Home." It would have been a book of our secret recipes for things like the SMELL of apple pie, pumpkin bread, fresh laundry or spring cleaning. Our motto would be, "Get the Smell Without the Work!" Alone, the recipe for the smell of apple

111

pie could have been worth a fortune! The time it would save busy homemakers was priceless. Our instructions would be clear:

Purchase an apple pie from you favorite bakery. Remove the pie from its cardboard box. (Burn the box or discard it in the neighbor's garbage can.) Place the pie in your own pie tin. Note: Bakery pies are usually 8", while most household pie tines are 9". If the store-bought pie is smaller than your tin, simply smash the pastry down until it fits, giving it an even more genuine "homemade" look.

Meanwhile, combine the following:

- 1 Tblsp. flour
- 1 Tblsp. cooking oil
- 1 Tblsp. water
- 1 Tsp. each: cloves, nutmeg and cinnamon
- 1 apple core

Mix ingredients in a disposable tin (chicken pot pie size). Shove the apple core into the center of the dough and bake at 225 degrees, all day. (For the smell of pumpkin pie on Thanksgiving, substitute a chunk of the Jack-o-lantern still on the front porch from Halloween, for the apple core.)

Was it our fault that we had so much fun while we worked? Maybe some things just weren't fair. Back home, at least, they weren't, and I was about to show my husband my new ideas for changing things on the homefront. Perhaps what I wanted, almost more than a 50/50 deal, was appreciation for what I was doing to make our home an oasis from the world outside. I was doing more than Danny realized and, in his unknowingness, he had been insensitive. We continued our talk.

"So what else?" he said.

"Have you noticed how neat the house has been lately?" I asked.

"Yes, I have and I've wondered how long it will last."

Wanting to rip his tongue out, but containing myself for a more productive victory, I deliberately put down my nail file, folded my hands and proceeded to explain our new infraction game. With a feeling of superiority, I presented him with his personal list of infractions for the last couple of days ($6.75 worth), reassuring him that it was merely a probationary week, so he needn't actually pay.

I showed him, in writing, how his messes contributed to the conditions he so disliked. It was the first time he was aware that HIS stuff was cluttering the house as much as an unpacked suitcase had. He had to admit that the object of the game (lowest infractee takes all) was a most brilliant money twist, and the by-product of a clutter-free house was even more appealing.

"So, Danny, do I have your support?"

"You sound like a Bartles and James commercial. Sure, I'll play."

With clutter out of the way, we moved on to the more delicate issue of his contribution to household responsibilities. I got to say all the things I had practiced on my sister and rehearsed in my mind. I didn't leave out a word, and I had his complete attention when I said, "It is no longer men's work or women's work! It is people-who-live-in-the-house work!" At one point, I had to ask Danny to relax his lips from an angry line and unfold his arms. He asked me to stop pointing at him and to contralto my voice.

"Can I read something to you?" I was holding some papers in my hand. "It's about Christmas." He had a pained look on his face, as if he were about to listen to an Edgar Allan Poe poem.

"Sure."

"It's a list of all the things that, traditionally, have fallen in my lap." He listened as I read all the things that had to be done:

- Make a list of the holiday and family traditions to be followed
- Take the children to see Santa Claus
- Go caroling
- Find out what children and family members want for Christmas
- Make gift list for family, friends, neighbors, colleagues, employees, children's gifts to family, friends,and teachers
- Select gifts that must be mailed early
- Buy gifts that must be mailed early
- Take children shopping so that they can pick out their presents for each other, parents, grandparents and teachers
- Mail the gifts
- Buy remainder of gifts (including extra gifts for

those you forgot who might drop in)
- Buy stocking stuffers
- Buy wrapping paper, ribbons, gift cards and tape
- Wrap the gifts
- Make card list (save for next year)
- Buy cards
- Address cards
- Buy stamps
- Mail early
- Rearrange furniture
- Order tree
- Pick up tree
- Buy and hang wreath
- Check decorations (creche, tree stand)
- Check tree lights (replace bulbs)
- Make decorations (string popcorn and cranber-ries, make tree ornaments)
- Buy decorations (bulbs, tinsel, hooks)
- Trim the tree
- Clean the house
- Buy and arrange holly, mistletoe, flowers and pine bows
- Set up the candles
- Decorate the house (yard and outside the house)
- Place gifts under the tree
- Hang and stuff stockings
- Leave a snack for Santa near the tree
- Give tips, gifts, thanks and appreciation to special

people (milkman, mailman, paper boy, employees, garbage collector, hair dresser)

- Check after-holiday sales on Christmas gifts for next year.
- Remember the needy and donate to your favorite charity

"And now, Danny, you're finished, unless, of course, like last year, we're going to have another Christmas party. Then you need to:

- Decide on the date and the time
- Plan the guest list
- Write out directions to the house and duplicate it
- Call the guests
- Buy the stamps
- Send out the invitations and directions
- Plan the menu
- Make shopping list
- Order special holiday food (goose, seafood, plum pudding)
- Access the needs for a caterer or other help and hire
- Borrow/rent/buy tables, chairs, coat rack, bar, coffee maker
- Wash/borrow/rent/buy/ dishes, cups, serving dishes and punch bowl
- Wash/borrow/rent/buy glasses (wine, champagne, eggnog, punch)
- Polish/borrow/rent/buy silverware
- Polish trays and silver items (candlesticks and candy dishes)

- Clean table linens, dish towels and aprons
- Take out the napkin rings
- Refill salt and pepper shakers
- Prepare an outfit to be worn
- Check recipes for procedures to be done in advance
- Buy ingredients for special holiday treats (fruitcakes, candy and cookies)
- Buy holiday candles
- Buy the beverages
- Replenish the bar with condiments and supplies (onions, olives, cherries, lemons, limes, oranges and stirrers)
- Buy mixers and juices
- Buy film and flash bulbs
- Buy paper goods (paper towels, napkins and toilet paper)
- Shop for the food
- Get money to cover all the expenses
- Make the ice
- Chill the beverages
- Make a list of cooking and serving chores
- Make holiday drinks (eggnogs and toddies)
- Prepare foods that can be made ahead of time
- Put out the guest towels
- Clear out the closet and set up a coat rack
- Prepare a place for boots and umbrellas
- Check outdoor lighting

- Load the camera
- Put out ashtrays and coasters
- Buy last-minute perishables
- Buy the flowers and make a centerpiece
- Cook
- Set the table
- Put out the ice bucket, tongs, condiments and snacks
- Make the juices for the drinks
- Decant the wine
- Set up the coffee maker and the teapot
- Prepare the sugar bowl, creamer, lemons and tea bags
- Put out the ice
- Heat up the toddies
- Set out the hors d'oeuvres
- Warm and prepare the serving dishes
- Serve and clean as you go
- Clean up
- Return the rented/borrowed items

"See, I do Christmas every year, and your part is licking envelopes! That's not fair."

"I guess not, but I can tell you, we'll never have another Christmas party! That's insanity!"

"And listen to this. There's another list for packing for a summer vacation..."

Okay! Okay! Okay! I get the picture. What do you want

me to do?"

"I want you to do your half."

It was the beginning of new awareness for my husband and, from that time on, things were very different. I designed new 3x5 housekeeping cards that divided the household work more fairly (to be explained in detail in Chapter Eight) and, with our Infraction game, our home finally was that oasis we all wanted.

In the next weeks, we would redefine the game to cover gray areas such as personal bedrooms. In the name of relaxation, the resident needed to be able to kick back and leave out a little, but we agreed that no laundry, dishes, trash or unmade beds would be allowed.

To keep the children from nosing around each other's bedrooms and our own, in search of violations, we added an invasion-of-privacy clause, whereby minors were not permitted to infract anything in another person's bedroom. Only parental tagging in those rooms would be permitted.

We learned, in time, that if the infraction cards came down, so did the house. As embarrassing as it was, the degree of neatness in our home depended on the 3x5's on the bulletin board. We were accountable because of cash, but at least we were accountable.

(We also discovered that, if the losers didn't fork over the money within 24 hours, they got away without paying, because everybody was concentrating on the next week's game. We made a new rule to stop the boys from cheating their sister out of her due. If payment, in cash, wasn't received within 24 hours of the verified tally, players would owe double the amount, compounded daily.)

With Danny's input, the game was even more fun. We continued to make new rulings, like time-outs for illness, holidays and vacations, and 72-hour amnesty for school books left out during finals. A shower lasting more than seven minutes was declared a misdemeanor, stopping hot-water hogs cold!

After playing the game for several weeks, we added the car and the yard...and Styrofoam meat trays in the driveway were a thing of the bitter past.

Memories From
Our Album

Terry, Joanna, Peggy, Pam and Michael
September 25, 1988

Allyson, Jeff, Danny, Peggy and Chris.

Peggy at the beach with her new car

Dad, Mom, Pam and Terry at Timberline Lodge on the wedding day

Two house guests at Peggy's home
One napping, the other leaping

Baby Chelsea Marie

Bad boy Dorothy Young

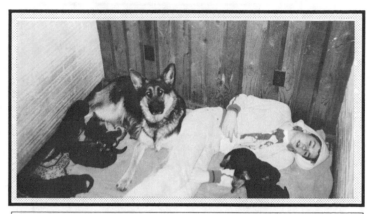

Peggy's laundry room, converted into a nursery

Chelsea Marie in her backyard

Our assistant, Dee Anne, with Pam in front of a big red nine we found in New York

Peggy, Sonya Friedman and Pam

Peggy, Lily Tomlin and Pam

Pam, Teri Garr and Peggy on the set at AM Los Angeles

*Peggy, Sally
Jessy Raphael
and Pam*

Pam, Dennis Weaver and Peggy on a TV set in Houston

Ted McGinley, excited about reading
**The Sidetracked Sister's Catch-Up on the
Kitchen**

Mother's Day preparations just before dialing 911

Chef Jones making his "barbecue dip" for the Mother's Day feast

Chef Young preparing his part of the "filler"

133

The mothers playing
"Ball in the Pants"

134

The sparkling cider is poured

Dinner is served

The Mother's Day Cleanup

Tired, but pleased with themselves

All for one and one for all

Chapter Six

Keeping Up With The Joneses

Before I decided to try the infraction cards at my house, I watched Peggy and her family for more than four months. It was amazing how consistently tidy her house was. Each person had taken responsibility for his or her own belongings, and Danny had assumed a good portion of the household tasks. The yard, which had always looked good, was even neater because the whole family was doing their part in it.

It was summer now, and I was back to being a single mother with three children in the house. Mike and Peggy Ann were home from college and busy with their summer jobs. I knew if I didn't get control soon, I would once again experience a summer full of stress. I'd barely made it through spring break with a voice.

Terry did call me back after he had rested from dinner

at my house, and we started seeing each other almost every day.

We had met when we were 13. We'd gone through junior high school and high school together and, although we had never dated, we had always been good friends. We were cheerleading partners for three years in high school and spent hours with each other, practicing our routines with the rally squad. We were together every Friday night because there was always a game. Our scrapbooks have many pictures of us together...because we always were. Now we were spending wonderful hours, remembering our happy days and planning new ones.

One night we were having dinner in a very romantic setting, discussing how compatible we were, when he said something that abruptly changed the tone of the evening.

"I can see that there is a slight difference in the way you live and the way I do." He looked as if he hoped I was listening.

"Really, and what is that?" I could feel a judgment coming my way, and I silently reminded myself that I take criticism very easily.

"I have noticed that you and your kids leave quite a bit of stuff out at your house." Mysteriously, he seemed to look like my mother for an instant.

Even though I knew it was generally true, I wanted him to be specific. "Like what, for instance?"

"Oh, like the blanket Joanna took when we went to watch the fireworks. It's August. The blanket has been in the entry way for over three weeks."

I suddenly knew how my sister had felt when she and Danny had had their huge fight. "Terry, that blanket is 100 percent wool, so I have to take it to the cleaners. I keep telling myself I have to go there, and then I get busy and forget. Since it's been out so long, I don't see it any more and, besides, Chelsea Marie is using it for a bed now." He seemed to understand.

I told him I really didn't think that the messy house would be a problem between us, because it had been bothering me for a couple of months and I intended to change things. I explained, rather defensively, that our book, *SIDETRACKED HOME EXECUTIVES,* was wonderful for organizing household cleaning chores. I pointed out that my house was immaculate as far as the floors, windows, bathrooms, woodwork and everything else was concerned. He agreed that was true, and he seemed to be relieved that I was aware of the other problem. Grateful that the discussion was over, we let the candlelight and music regain their magic hold on us.

Spurred by the stimulating dinner conversation the night before and impressed with my sister's successful cleanup campaign, I decided I'd try the infraction game on MY family. Since Peggy had told me that during the first week they played the game, she hadn't really charged the money, I decided to do the same thing.

I went through the house with five infraction cards (one for each person and one for listing items that would be a

141

question mark) and about fifty bright red dots. Instead of tagging something, putting the time on the dot, waiting an hour and then writing the infraction on the card, I decided to dot and infract at the same time. I figured that, since I wasn't going to charge money for the first week, there was no need to give anyone an hour to put his or her things away.

In fifteen minutes I had filled up all the cards and had to write on the back of Mike's and mine. I put a dot on everything I could see that should be put away.

I discovered during the dotting process that, like the Fourth of July blanket, many of my belongings hadn't seemed like clutter to me. I had become oblivious to the fact that they contributed to the over-all messiness of the house. The rule in Peggy's home was, "If it isn't decorative, it isn't out." I had to be very careful to be objective with my own belongings, so I had to ask myself if my pocket calculator was really that pretty on the kitchen counter. Was the world globe that attractive in the bathroom? (That room had the best light in the house, and Joanna and I had taken the awkward ball in there to examine Indonesia with my magnifying glass.) Were my shoes an accent under the lamp table? Was my purse a nice touch, hanging on the dining room chair?

When I finished dotting everything, the house looked like somebody weird lived there. Adding up all the infractions at 25 cents each, there was a total of $14.75 we would have to pay if this wasn't the probationary week.

I didn't put away any of my stuff, because I wanted the

kids to know that this was a problem we all needed to work on, including me. I couldn't wait for each of them to get home from work so I could show them what I'd done.

When I get a new idea in my head, whether I think it up myself or get it from somebody else, I lose all my sense of timing. Invariably, I prematurely jump into sharing before the sharee has a chance to think. Like the time I came home from Weight Watchers and shared the water rule I had learned, with my sister. Marilyn, the group leader, had told us that she had lost 120 pounds in 14 months and, in the few weeks that she didn't have a weight loss, she could directly attribute it to NOT drinking the eight glasses of water Weight Watchers recommends.

When I told Peggy about that, she said she and Danny would try to follow the rule. Later she told me that Danny had bucked the idea because he said he'd feel like a fool, filling an eight-ounce glass at the drinking fountain in the police station.

I knew there had to be a solution. A couple of weeks later, as I was drinking one of my waters, I got the idea to count the gulps it took to finish the glass. It took 15 gulps. I immediately called Peggy and passed on the information. She called Danny and he said he'd try out my idea.

It wasn't until the next day that I found out he was mad at me. She said that he had had trouble the day before, drinking so much water. He had called her from work and complained that he couldn't leave the station for very long, because he had to keep going to the bathroom. Peggy had told him that I had said that, when you first start drinking the amount of water you need, it will seem like too much because you aren't used to consuming the proper amount.

The next morning while he was standing at the sink, drinking his first glass of the day, Danny had inadvertently started counting his gulps. It seems it only took five swallows and the glass was empty! How was I to know that people's gulpers are different? We figured that Danny must have drunk about forty glasses of water that day. It was no wonder he couldn't leave the police station.

This new game idea was far more exciting than gulping water, and I could hardly wait for the kids to get home. As usual, my timing was terrible.

Mike came home first. Just as soon as he was through the door, I nailed him. I didn't give him a chance to unwind and cool off from the summer heat; I slapped the infraction card in his face like a ticket-happy cop and started in on him.

"Mike, things are going to change around here and I'm starting with you. This is what you call an infraction card. It's got your name on the top, and your sisters and I each have one of our own. I went around the house today and I found 27 clutter violations on you alone! That comes to six dollars and seventy-five cents!"

"What? Why?"

"Each infraction costs twenty-five cents, but I'm not going to charge you anything yet. You'll have a week of probation. But just look at this." I handed him the official-looking infraction card. "There are dish, glass, spoon and fork infractions, some dirty underwear violations, and some miscellaneous messes like the shaving stuff you left out. That one mess alone would have cost you one dollar and twenty-five cents!"

"Mom, chill out!"

"Do what?"

"Chill."

"Don't get sassy with me, Michael. This is my house and, if you are going to stay here, you will have to live by the rules! From now on, nothing will be left out unless it's decorative. That means your briefcase and backpack are out of the living room. That also means if you eat a piece of pie and you don't clean up after yourself, it will cost you a dollar and a quarter. A quarter for the knife you used to cut the pie, a quarter for the plate, a quarter for the fork, a quarter for the glass of milk you drank to wash the pie down, and a quarter for the crumbs you left when you cut the pie.

"See, what you'll do is, when you cut a piece of pie, you'll put the knife in the dishwasher. Then when you pour your-self a glass of milk, you'll put the milk carton away. Then you'll eat the piece of pie, drink the milk and put the dish, fork and glass in the dishwasher with the knife. Then you'll brush the crumbs off of the kitchen counter into your hand and throw the crumbs into the garbage can under the sink. No, on second thought, you'll clean up the crumbs BEFORE you eat the pie. Oh! and if the bag under the sink just happens to be full, you'll empty it in the garbage can in the garage." I was out of breath.

"Mom, is there pie?"

"No, that was just an example of a typical mess I end up cleaning up. I'm not going to do it any more. I'm sick and tired of being everyone's slave. Oh, I almost forgot. If you have friends over, you will be responsible for their messes. I can think of one particular night of entertainment that would have cost you about eleven thousand dollars!"

"Mom, it's 102 degrees outside. Could I get out of this suit before I clean up my stuff?"

"Yes, but after this week there will be a time written on an infraction dot. The rule at Aunt Peg's house is that you have an hour from the time you are dotted."

Peggy Ann came home next. She had been working at Super Tan as a receptionist.

"Peggy, this is called an infraction card. On it is a list of items you've left out. It adds up to five dollars and fifty cents."

"Mom, I'm sunburned, and you know I don't have five dollars and fifty cents. Besides, you didn't give me any warning!"

"I won't start charging for a week."

"How am I supposed to pay after a week is up? I have to save my money for college!"

"Well, maybe you'll have to quit school."

I explained the rules in detail to her, and I had one more kid to go. I waited for Joanna to get home from her babysitting job. She was the least guilty of messes, since she was born organized. She came in around 5:30 and plopped down on the couch with a growl.

"Oh, those Hinds kids! What a couple of brats! Mom, you wouldn't believe how awful they are! The parents don't believe in saying no! Jamie got mad at me because she wanted to watch cartoons and I was watching "Days," so she went over and pulled the cat's tail. Sometimes when she gets mad at me, she takes it out on the cat. So I go, 'Don't be mean to the cat!' and she goes, 'She likes it,' and I go, 'She does not.' Then Mark comes in and he flicks the TV while we're arguing. Oh, Mom, I don't know how I'm going to last the whole summer over there."

"Joanna, I'm sorry, but I have to change the subject for a sec. This is an infraction card. Notice your name is on it. So far today, you owe one dollar and fifty cents. You left out your manicure stuff, and you need to take the blanket that's in the hall and put it out in the car. I'm going to take it to the cleaners."

"Mom, that's not fair. Mike and Peg have junk out all over the house."

"I know that, and from now on it's going to cost them."

When I explained how the new system worked, I could see the money light go on in her little blond head. Her natural ability to keep things neat would now pay off in cash.

The system soon worked wonders in our house and, if it hadn't been for my lousy timing, it would have been an almost perfect transition.

It was not surprising that in that first week of playing the game, I was the one with the most infractions. Mike was a close second, Peggy Ann was third and, of course, Joanna would have won the pot.

I have to say there were quite a few fights at the refrigerator where the infraction cards were taped. When you are guilty, it's very hard to find out that you have been written up for something, but it makes you nuts to be written up when you are innocent. A good example was the time Mike wrote Peggy up for leaving a cereal bowl in the sink. Peggy was innocent, so she crossed through the infraction notation with a bold line and wrote, "NO WAY!". Then she turned her vengeful pen onto Joanna's infraction card and wrote her up for the bowl. By the end of the day, the children's cards were severely defaced by the duelling pens, and the cereal bowl was mine.

We had to make a rule that NO ONE was allowed to cross off an infraction without a group hearing. It's a good idea to have a "question mark" infraction card so that, if there is doubt about an item, it can be written up and dealt with later.

I discovered that, just as at Peggy's house, if the infraction cards were not posted every week, the house would fall back into a state of chaos. It was maddening to think that a few stupid little three-by-five cards and some fluorescent red dots stood between clutter and order, but it was wonderful to realize that those simple tools could bring order out of chaos!

148

Chapter Seven

From Chauvinist To Domestic Champion

After seeing some miraculous, overnight family cooperation and spousal enlightenment on the homefront, we knew that we had to share our experiences. Unfortunately, when we began promoting our new ideas in workshops, we were severely off course on one thing. We thought that every married woman would have to FIGHT for cooperation, and we encouraged it!

Because of Peggy's horrible fight, Danny was a changed man! Although he wasn't ready to teach a home ec class, he was certainly in line for an 'A' in the effort department.

One day, while sitting in his chair in the living room, with one of his cats at his feet and a black guest cat in his lap (he had consented to let a couple of cats from Hollywood live with the family while their owner, a long-time friend, was out of the country for two weeks), he told us how pleased he was with the strides he had made.

He started counting his domestic achievements on his right hand. "I make the bed every morning; I do laundry and even sort correctly; I make my own lunch and I fix breakfast every Saturday!" When he had used up the fingers on one hand, he stopped petting the napping boarder and continued until he had all ten fingers out. "I can iron; I can clean shrimp..." when he finished, he looked so proud of his new-found talents, and we still have that picture of him engraved in our minds.

With a feeling of superiority, Danny was actively fanning the flames of our little, grass roots ERA movement on the homefront. We were amazed at how adamant he was that other men should follow his example. "Hey, these male chauvinists better get a clue! Just today this clown at work was bragging about his wife. 'She'll do anything for me! A woman's place is in the home, cookin', cleanin' the house, raisin' the kids and takin' care of her husband. Her place is not out there makin' more money than me! A woman is supposed to support the man and be there when he needs her.'

It's that kind of a guy I'd like to see hung up by the fruit of his looms! And you two are just the ones to do it! Ya know, there are gonna be some male chauvinists who'll be left lying in the dirt after this is all over. I give you guys a lot of credit for having the courage to stand up and be willing to take the heat you'll get for starting all of this." We felt influential and confident that we were right to encourage women to fight.

If a good marriage, like Peggy's, had to endure a four-day battle before order and a fair dispersal of the work load could be established, it only seemed logical that any woman who wanted a 50/50 deal out of her mate would have to go on the warpath and be ready for a confrontation at least as critical as Peggy's and Danny's. Since Pam was single, she didn't have to face off with another adult in order to start plastering dots everywhere and infracting unaware victims.

Based on what had happened to Peggy, we concluded that the single woman would be the ONLY one who wouldn't have to fight. We thought that Peggy's and Danny's stand-off was inevitable for all married couples who were not equally sharing the work.

When the infraction idea had been successfully keeping our homes in order for almost a year, it was the beginning of 1988. Sexual politics had become a volatile issue. Women were extremely angry, and men were the target of their wrath. Bookshelves were sagging with best-sellers convicting men of everything from infidelity to impotency. Shere Hite hit the circuit with her venomous column of controversial evidence, indicting men as jerks, and every television and radio talk show was focusing on the hot controversy.

Meanwhile, journalists were busy exposing the deeds of sleazy males in the news. Jimmy Swaggart, Gary Hart and Jim Bakker were all caught with their pants down, striking a heavy blow at masculine propriety and plunging the reputation of men in general farther into the hole. Women were rightfully pointing an accusatory finger at the opposite sex, and we couldn't help getting caught up in the fever of feminine hostility.

While women were in a fit of aggravation, men were in a state of confusion. A man was not quite sure if it was appropriate to open a door for a woman, light her cigarette or pay for her dinner. At least, he had learned that a "friendly" slap on the butt in the office would inevitably get a sexual harassment suit slapped in his face. Outside the home, men were being flown by women pilots, arrested by women cops, tried by women lawyers and sentenced by women judges. They were having to mind women employers, salute women generals and cough for women doctors.

The timing for a declaration of war on the homefront seemed appropriate because men were on the defensive. The issue of equality for women was not a new subject, but the issue of equality in the home was. We concluded that, with a surprise attack from their wives (who would be revved up and ready to fight after hearing our battle cry), men all over our nation would finally be willing to share the housework with their mates.

In February, 1988, we were asked to be guests on "Geraldo" to discuss the question, "Who does the Housework?" We jumped at the chance to expose inequalities on the homefront. We arrived in New York with a battlefield strategy to get husbands to do half of all household responsibilities, including child care. Geraldo Rivera had filled his audience with couples willing to tell how they shared the work load in their homes. Of an audience of about 200, three women alleged that their husbands did half. However, by the end of the show, after hearing the extent of what really had to be done to keep the household running smoothly, they realized that their mates weren't even CLOSE to doing half. The rest of the women in the audience were furious about the dilemma they faced.

Our solution was a 13-step program that included, of course, a fight. We explained on national television that, as painful as it might be, women would have to face the fact that there would have to be a showdown to get men to change. We even went as far as to say that, if a woman was unable to get her husband to see the light (after enlisting the help of a marriage counselor), she might have to take step number 13 and get a good attorney!

By the end of the hour, all the women were angry with their husbands and all the men were mad at us. We came back to Salmon Creek and Hazel Dell, feeling pleased about the revolution we had stirred. We thought there had been a real breakthrough.

Meanwhile, in our speeches to churches and women's groups, we were telling audiences how important it was for women to stand up for their rights. We shared the 13-step program with thousands of people, telling them about the inevitable fight they would have to have in order to achieve equality. Women wholeheartedly agreed with what we were saying. We preached that, until we had equality in our homes, women could forget about having a woman president or having a Congress that was half female. We said that, until we raised a generation of people, both male and female, who would respect women enough to vote for them, we were not going to see the equality America truly stood for.

We would start every speech with the question: "How many of you feel that you and your husband share the work equally in your home?" In an audience of 500, there would always be three or four women who would raise their hands. Then we'd pose this question: "How many of you carry most of the domestic burden?" The audience would look like a wheat field ready for harvest. After a typical two-hour speech, which seemed always to turn into a rally of zealous females, we'd ask, "How many of you would like to change the way housework is divided up in your home?" EVERYBODY'S hand would shoot up. Then, much to our dismay, when we asked the final question, "How many of you are going to go home and fight for the change?" no one...NO ONE... would raise her hand.

We knew, judging by our own feelings, that most women hate confrontation, but we honestly believed that, if they thought that the results of an all-out war against inequality would achieve peace and harmony, most women would be willing to fight. THEY AREN'T! But we weren't quite ready to accept that.

We were confused about what to do with women who were not going to jump in and act on what they obviously agreed was a major problem. We had stirred something in them all right, but, for their own personal reasons, they were willing to walk out of the auditorium and go back to their homes, status quo.

Terry, who has a good marketing sense, was troubled to hear that, at the end of our speeches, women were not responding to the war drums by purchasing our 50/50 Family Kit, complete with printed Infraction Cards and two Strategy Cassettes.

"If the women in your audience aren't willing to commit to a fight, why would you think they would buy any of your fighting tools?" Terry asked. "And besides, YOUR idea of a fight and some other woman's idea may be totally different. In a lot of cases, it's not going to be a matter of the guy losing his lips like you say Danny and I do. It'll be the woman losing her teeth! I suggest you analyze your market more closely and pinpoint your target customer."

With that in mind, after speaking to a typical audience of corporate spouses at their convention, we took Terry's advice and came up with a profile of three kinds of women.

We found the extremely militant woman, who came into the world with a cloud over her head, a knife between her teeth, and a man under her thumb. She was ready to go for the throat of anyone who wasn't fair. She was tough and battle-scarred, and she would DEMAND equality in her life. She could probably write a book called, "The Joy of Confrontation." We thought she might buy our battlefield program just for the fun of it.

Then there was the other extreme: a woman who wouldn't make a move without her husband's permission. She was subservient, down-trodden and submissive, and she was resigned to stay in her security zone of dependency, even at the expense of losing her self. If she did buy the material, she'd have to hide it some place where her husband would never find it (such as the laundry room).

What was left was the majority of reasonable women, who fell into the category in between. They definitely wanted a change, but hadn't gained the courage to take a stand. THEY WERE OUR TARGET CUSTOMERS, but we had failed to convince any of them to fight for what they wanted. We didn't know what to do with that information.

Ignoring the response from our audiences, we were spurred on by Danny's transformation, along with his powerful military backing. In March, we submitted a book proposal to John Boswell, our literary agent, *50/50 ON THE HOMEFRONT: BATTLEFIELD STRATEGIES TO GET HUSBANDS TO DO HALF*. It had a definite militant tone with chapter titles such as: Get Mad And Get Even, Wisdom On The Warpath, Blueprint For Battle, Declaration Of War and The Aftermath. John said it wouldn't work.

He was right. Soon we began receiving the fall-out from the bomb we had dropped on Geraldo's show. Sad letters from defeated women started drifting into our office. They said things like "I had the fight and now he's gone."

We weren't prepared to handle the woman who would fight, lose and regret that she had ever taken our advice. Since the guy was gone, it was too late to ask him to play the Infraction game (which, in the interest of time, had not been mentioned on the show). The only consolation we could offer was that everything works out for the best, and in the end, maybe she was better off without him. (Not very comforting at the time, but probably true.)

In the aftermath of the war we had perpetrated, we decided to recall all of our battlefield tapes, cancel our militant workshops and throw out our 13-step fight plan, before we wrecked any more marriages and felt responsible for the overcrowded battered women's shelters.

We concluded that a fight wouldn't be necessary as long as the couple had our peaceful solution, and the husband would be willing to be a good sport.

It wasn't until mid-summer of 1988 that we found out why the Infraction game really worked. The light certainly didn't come on in either of our heads. What we learned, we agreed, could only have come from a man.

While we were talking to John Boswell one morning, discussing how to get the spirit of war out of the book we were proposing, he asked, "Why do you really think the game works so well?" We both said it was the money that spawned such enthusiasm.

He laughed. "Do you mean to tell me that you think a 40-year-old man is inspired by a pot of change at the end of a week?" We had to admit that that did sound a little stupid.

"You guys really don't know, do you?"

"Well, then, if you're so smart, why DOES it work?"

"Competition. It's plain and simple...COMPETITION!"

We had to think about that for awhile. It was true that

157

competition was half of it, but we realized that there was more....The other half was GOOD SPORTSMANSHIP!

From the time men are little boys (and we know this from rearing three of them ourselves), they are taught to be good sports, and they will do nearly anything to prove that they are. Competition is inherent in the genes of every American male. It's the sport of it and, in any competition, "good sports" play by the rules.

Ice hockey is a good example. We went to a game once and thought it was hysterical that tough, aggressive athletes would be willing to sit in a naughty box for breaking a rule by being too wild. There isn't a man alive, in his right mind, who would consent to sit somewhere in a pen, as a punishment for being unruly, unless it was one of the rules of the game.

Call it good sportsmanship and you can get eleven tough men to stop frantically grappling for an elusive football...just by throwing a hanky into the air. Call it good sportsmanship and nine giant men will stand with their toes exactly on the line, while the player who was roughed up gets one or two chances to throw a ball through a ring without anybody messing with him.

Call it a game and a man will pay thousands of dollars to be part of an elite club, wear special clothes and drive a popsicle-type truck all over several hundred acres of grassland, smacking a little dimpled ball toward designated holes in the lawn. In the name of good sportsmanship, the same man who leaves his dirty tracks across a newly waxed kitchen floor will actually stop his game and rake his footprints out of a patch of sand he's had to walk through to whack his ball out of the grains.

Sportsmanship at home! That was it! It was competition and being a good sport that motivated each person in the family, especially the man of the house, to play by "the new house rules of order." We think that, on the playing fields, competition motivates athletes to win, because they hate to lose. We also think that the rules for good sportsmanship were invented because the athletes wouldn't play fair without them. If we were right, then our home Infraction game would work with anyone who loves that "Wide World of Sports."

Danny wasn't just proud of his home ec skills; he felt a superiority over all the flunky male homemakers in America. He was truly a domestic champion!

Chapter Eight

𝒯𝒽𝑒 50/50 𝒻𝑎𝓂𝒾𝓁𝓎

Once your husband realizes how important HE is to the success of a messless house, you are on your way to a 50/50 family.

Our definition of a 50/50 family is one in which the husband and wife stand together as an example of cooperation. To be that wonderful example to the children, the mother and father, if they both work outside of the home, must spend an equal share of time and energy on household maintenance and childcare. That doesn't mean that one week the husband cleans the toilet and takes the kids to ballet lessons, and the next week the wife does it. It means that the couple is more aware of the time and energy each spends working at home, and there is a sincere attempt to share the enormous burden, equally.

Today about 50 percent of all marriages end in divorce. Statistics show that it is usually the woman who throws in the towel, along with all the rest of the laundry. Judging by most of the people we know who have divorced, we think that almost all of those marriages probably could have been saved. Perhaps the truth behind courtroom scenes is that the couples aren't as overwrought with each other as they are with their SITUATIONS. When a situation gets out of hand, it's easy to lose your perspective and confuse the two.

If the house is a mess and all you do is complain and whine, pretty soon no one listens to you. Everyone knows how long you'll nag before you explode, and they'll ride your fuse to the wire. If you choose to keep quiet and pick up after everyone yourself, you end up feeling like a martyr. Your resentment escalates and, before you know it, you are a cranky, exhausted lump of nagging humanity. You feel as if nobody cares. You look at your husband and children in anger instead of understanding. You feel a sense of futility.

The good news is that being upset with a situation is far less critical than being upset with a person, because you can change situations. Homes CAN become neat, and stay that way. When a house is orderly and the woman is no longer solely responsible for making it that way, she will then have more energy to be fun-loving, kind and nurturing.

We said previously that a house, even if it is cleaned regularly, will still seem dirty, if the people who live in it are not accountable for their messes. Our solution to the problem of messiness, described in this book, is very good, but it doesn't address the janitorial needs in a home. The 3x5 cardfile system that we developed and explained in our first book, "SIDETRACKED HOME EXECUTIVES", in 1977, is the answer to that one.

It was inspired by a rotating tickler file system that Peggy had to use when she worked at our local newspaper, selling display advertising.

On her first day of work, her supervisor gave her a little recipe file box filled with index cards. There was a client's name on each card, along with his address, phone number and information on how often he advertised. There were also dividers, Monday through Friday, for each day of the week.

On Monday, Peggy would go to the file and pull out all of the cards for that day. She would prioritize them and call the most important advertisers first. At the end of the day, if she hadn't called Squeezer's Dairy (he didn't advertise very much), she would skip Squeezer (note it on his card) and file him for a later date. Peggy said, "All of those little advertisers just kept going around and around in the box and, since I mind really well, I called every one of them regularly."

When we decided to get organized back in 1977, Peggy had remembered that she "...was organized once! At the newspaper, anyway." She explained how the system worked and we agreed that housework is repetitive....Well, it is if you do it.

With that new thought, we made a list of all the jobs that had to be done regularly in our houses. We bought dividers, one through 31, for the days of the month, and reams of 3x5 cards.

Through the years we have perfected the system, and our NEW job cards are detailed in this book. (See the Appendix.) With our instructions, you will be able to fill out your own 3x5s, or you can order our printed cards, which have been especially designed for the two career family.

As we improved the system, we came up with a wonderful way to compensate our children for the housework they do.

Each job card has a time estimate in the right-hand corner. That number is the key to our point system. We assigned a point value to every job in our homes, according to how long the job takes. We made each point equivalent to one minute of help. For an example, if one of the cards says it takes 20 minutes to sweep the deck, that job is worth 20 points. We keep track of points on charts that are posted in a central place.

A chart (see an example of one of our charts in the Appendix) has a place for the person's name and columns for the description of the job (sweep the deck); the point value (20 points); parent verification (each job must be inspected by a parent and initialed); the date, and the balance forward. A running balance is kept so that at any time, it is very clear how many points a person has. The points are worth money, merchandise or special parental services.

No matter what the age of a child, there are things he or

she wants. Young children may want to have a friend spend the night or play at the park, go to the show or visit the zoo. Older children want the keys to the family car, or the keys to the family car or the keys to the family car. Since children are always going to want SOMETHING as long as they live in your home, then you have a perfect opportunity to teach them to help, in trade for what they want. This barter method impresses upon kids that life isn't free. There is a price for everything.

A value must be previously assigned to all of your services, so that when one is needed, your child knows how many points he or she must collect to afford that service. We post a list of services and their price. We charge 250 points for one of our children's friends to spend the night. (That service includes popping popcorn, renting a movie and fixing a midnight snack.) To go roller-skating is 175 points. Charging points for using the car was inspired by Hertz - and the teen is charged by the mile. You need to set your own value on services, based on how valuable the services are to your children, and it is very important to have it in writing!

If the points are cashed in for money, we decided that one cent per minute was sufficient payment for simple jobs. Sweeping the deck would be worth 20 cents if the sweeper wanted to convert his or her work to cash. Bigger jobs for bigger kids, such as washing the car, fixing dinner, mowing the lawn or cleaning the fireplace, would have a greater value than a penny a minute.

We have thought of several other ways children can rack up points. We give them for grades (A's are worth 500 points, B's are worth 300 points, and C's just mean that the child has the privilege of living in the home through the next semester). We also give bonus points for compliments our children get from adults. For instance, if someone says one of our children was kind and gracious on the telephone, that compliment is worth 25 points. If we ever catch one of our kids being nice to his or her sibling, we give bonus points.

Any jobs that are performed voluntarily are worth double-point value. (That concept teaches children to think of ways to help without being asked.) We also run specials! For a given month, we might declare that anyone who empties the garbage or cleans out the kitty litter box receives double-point value.

If you are like we are, you hate the idea of keeping track of information, but once you post these charts (and you stand strong against requests without earned points), your children will begin to see the value in keeping track of the information on their own.

This chart idea has several uses. We have a friend who decided to use it to track the behavior of the guy she had been going with for three years. She loved him, but the man was a work-aholic, and the relationship seemed to be stuck in the waist-deep piles of his workload.

She decided to keep a running balance of what he contributed to the relationship, the same way we keep track of our kids' job contributions.

In time it was clear that the beau wasn't committed to the relationship with the same quality of caring that our friend was. After charting him for several months on paper, she could see, in black and white, that the man spent very little time and energy enriching their relationship.

He received 250 points for remembering her birthday and another 100 points for giving her a card with a puppy on the cover, since she loved dogs. She gave him several hundred points for just being great company (the one day a week they saw each other). He lost 200 points when Valentine's Day came and he gave her a scraggly potted geranium with the Payless sticker still on the bottom of the plastic flower pot. (This man was not cheap. He had just run out of time and opted for a quick stop at any store he could find open.) He gained 350 points for fixing her dripping sink and 400 points whenever he said, "I love you," rather than "Me, too". Because she was usually the one to say it first, the courter only picked up 800 points.

He lost 2,000 points for not being with her when her dad had open-heart surgery, and 500 points for not calling to see how he was doing. He got docked another 1,500 points for letting her think he had gone to Germany for three weeks, when, in fact, he had stayed home and caught up on back work that all work-aholics always have. He lost points every time he waited until Friday to call for their one weekend date, and every time he was late, it cost him 100 points (which totalled 1,200 points over the three-month period she charted him). The chart went on and on, and in the end, even though she loved him, she broke up with him.

Life has a way of slipping away, and if it is not going in the direction you want it to, you could end up wasting your life in the hopes that someday things will change. Charting what is happening will put your life in a different perspective. You'll be able to better see just exactly what is happening in your life.

Our friend didn't show the man his point chart, because she met someone else, fell in love and ceased caring if the worker changed or not. The guy went away without the slightest clue that he was 3,550 points in the hole.

Perhaps if he had seen his behavior in writing, he would have had a desire to change, but as far as our friend knows, he is probably repeating the same neglectful behavior in his current relationship...if he has one.

We think one of the reasons that sports are big all over the world is because of the word, "point." If points were not bestowed in games, no one would care much about the activity taking place on the field or court or table or any other surface. If you think about it, points are really silly, and yet everybody keeps score. We ask the score, argue the score, flaunt the score, celebrate the score; and the only way to have a score is to keep track of points. What is a point, anyway? A point is a unit of value in the eye of the beholder.

We learned early in our business career, working together almost every day, that points were valuable to the two of us. We are always giving each other points for remembering things, points for knowing something the other one doesn't know, points for working longer than the other one, etc. We never keep track of those points on paper and we wouldn't know what to do with them if we did, but those little invisible units of value have given us a real, tangible energy that mysteriously accompanies appreciation.

For some reason it is not easy for many people to give or receive compliments. Maybe they don't know what to say or how to say it. It is also socially unacceptable to ask for compliments, even though most of us would love more recognition. For us, the points have turned into a wonderful way to recognize each other's value. Whenever either of us feels we have not received proper credit for something we have done, it is so much easier to say, "Hey, I need some points for that," than to say, "I need to be told how great I am for doing what I did."

We suggest that you take the chart on page 203 and reproduce several copies. Give one to each of your children and explain how the system works. If you are going to start infracting the people in your house, you might as well get them all started helping more with the housework at the same time.

In all three of our previous books, we said, "Establish order yourself first, and your family will follow your lead." That's a crock! Well, it's partly a crock. It is true that if you want to have things change in your house, it will help if you change some of **YOUR** messy habits, before you start involving your family. (Chances are good that you are one of the major contributors to the clutter and chaos in your home.)

We suggest that you spend at least a week, watching yourself. Before you get a bunch of colored dots and start slapping them on everything that isn't decorative, start mentally infracting yourself, and you'll end up becoming very aware of some of your careless habits. You might as well get a jump on your family. In that week, think about the new changes that are going to take place in your home, and watch your husband and children to observe their infractibility.

With a week of self-observation on your side, you'll be ready to present this new plan to your family. But one word of caution. Positioning is crucial and, just as our government spends years positioning itself for peace talks, you need to be very careful about the timing for yours. Your FIRST shot is going to be your BEST shot! Prepare for it. Have it in writing when you talk to your husband. Then the two of you can present it to the children as a united front.

We know that a 50/50 deal is a little unreasonable to expect, at least at first; but the trend is far more important than instant results. (A potato baked in the oven at 400 degrees for an hour is better than instant mashed potatoes cooked in the microwave for ten seconds.)

People really do not like change, especially if it means more work. Be patient and praise every bit of improvement you see in your family. There is nothing more effective than appreciation in speeding up the trend of cooperation.

The change that will take place in you will be especially wonderful. The time and energy you used to spend, trying to get cooperation, will now be there for you to use for more positive things. Your family will be amazed at what a different person you are. You won't be nagging anymore. You'll have leisure time to nap, play and relax, and you will be so surprised that at the end of the day you will actually have energy left over for romance.

Families are in a transitional time right now. The new direction must be toward more cooperation. If each member of your family can clearly see that the changes will benefit everyone, then a 50/50 family is definitely a possibility in your home.

Chapter Nine:

The Honeymooners

From Pam

In August, Terry (the produce terrorist) and I became formally engaged. We set the wedding date for December 10, 1988.

Since it was a second marriage for each of us, and we'd done the big church deal, complete with bridesmaids, ushers, flower girls, pew bows and ring bearers, we wanted to have something more simple this time.

Peggy wanted us to be married in her home, and we accepted her very generous invitation. I felt that it would be one of the most spiritual places I could ever pick for such an important, life-changing event. However, I couldn't stop picturing her working too hard and being up the entire night before the wedding, decking the halls and cleaning upholstery.

Terry and I wanted a very small affair, with just our families and a few close friends. When we first sat down to compile the list of guests, we came up with a conservative count of 43. In a few days the number somehow doubled to include friends in both of our business circles. Within a couple of weeks, names from the corners of our minds and the pages of our Roll-a-dexes climbed onto our once-modest list. Two weeks after that, the register had swelled beyond the capacity of Peggy's house. I could envision the structure, which is on the edge of a cliff, giving way to the weight of the 400 people!

Terry and I agreed that we had some major axing to do, and we had other problems besides the length of the guest list. What kind of a ceremony would it be?

We wanted our wedding to be spiritual, not religious. (I had found the church program for my first marriage, taped in a quilted scrapbook, alongside the marriage license that I had allowed to legally imprison me for 15 years. Printed inside were the vows we had repeated. I was disgusted with what I had promised my first husband. I didn't want to promise to OBEY Terry or hear him promise to CHERISH me. After all, I was not a slave or a priceless family heirloom.)

I didn't want somebody in a black robe to ask, "Who gives this woman to be this man's wife?" I was not a piece of property that could be passed from one man who owned

174

me to another one who soon would.

I did not want us to be pronounced "man and wife," since it was already obvious that Terry was male. I pointed out that no one would ever pronounce a couple "husband and woman"!

Terry was unwilling to change his last name, so he understood when I said that my last name would remain "Young." Which, for the record, leaves out my mother's maiden name, which is really her father's last name, which left out her mom's last name, which was really her mom's father's last name, which means no woman has EVER been recognized by any LAST name except the one attached to her by a man, who may or may not have been worthy to have his name carried on. Terry agreed with my feminist thoughts.

The traditional wedding ritual wouldn't work for us. This time we knew exactly what we wanted, and we decided to conduct the ceremony ourselves. The simplicity of the idea thrilled us both.

Paring down the guest list proved to be almost impossible and, as the idea of organizing the whole event - sending invitations, ordering flowers, choosing a caterer, selecting food, etc. - began to sink in, I remembered how much I dislike organizing things like that. Just the thought of making a "To Do" list made me tired, and I kept thinking about how much work Peggy would have to do. Just before my left brain was ready to explode with all of the busy plans, I had a right-brainstorm!

I called Terry at work and told him my plan.

"Terry, I have a great idea! Let's get married right away."

"Okay."

"We'll go to someplace like Timberline Lodge."

"Okay."

"We'll just invite family."

"Okay."

"And let's have it be a surprise!"

"Really? You won't be able to keep it a secret."

"Oh, yes, I will!" (We decided to tell our children, but keep it from the rest of the family.)

We liked the plan and set the date for Sunday, September 25, 1988.

Right away, Terry called the courthouse to see about getting a marriage license, and found out that our idea to conduct our own ceremony was illegal. Someone HAD to officiate.

I thought, 'Then why not go down to the courthouse by ourselves on Friday, September twenty-third, and get the legal part out of the way; treat it just like signing an earnest money agreement. That way we would still keep it a secret. We would be married in the eyes of the state of Washington, but as far as WE were concerned, we wouldn't consider ourselves married until our family pronounced us husband and wife on September twenty-fifth, at Timberline Lodge'.

176

Keeping a secret from my sister was the hardest thing I have ever done. Several times I almost told her, but every time, I'd hear Terry say "You won't be able to keep it a secret." Peggy and I worked together every day, and in between work we talked wedding plans (December tenth wedding plans).

To make sure that she and her family would be available for the real wedding, I told her that Terry had received a huge bonus and wanted to take everyone out to breakfast to celebrate. She said it sounded like a nice idea, but she worried about the expense. She suggested that her kids stay home. I lied and told her that it was the biggest bonus any of us had ever seen. I told her that money was no object and that without her kids, it just wouldn't be the same. She bought it.

On Friday, Terry and I sneaked down to the courthouse at three o'clock. We pulled a witness off of the street and made him watch, as we signed the license. Then we waited in line, with 20 other couples, for the judge to call our number.

The experience was degrading. It made me so glad that Terry and I were alone, so that no one in our family had to be a part of the matrimonial cattle call.

The judge was ready for a different bench...one in the park. He was confused when we told him that we did not want to make any big deal on this "leg" of our marriage. We wanted him to be brief. He wasn't. He recited an endless formal script, forgot parts and had to re-track himself, called me Pamellia, and lectured us about being so blase during the whole thing. (Terry and I had agreed that the transaction should be as sterile as possible, so we didn't even kiss when the robed magistrate told us to.)

When the paperwork was complete, it was 6:30 p.m.. Terry went to his apartment, and I raced over to my sister's house to stay with her kids. (She and Danny were away on an overnight business trip, but they had assured me that they would be home in time for the "breakfast" at Mt. Hood.)

"Surprises are 75% enjoyed by the surpriser, and 25% by the surprisee." Peggy Jones, September 25, 1988.

When we were all seated at the breakfast table, Terry proposed a toast.

"I'd like to announce that, right after we finish breakfast, Pam and I are going to be married, and we want all of you to be a part of it."

My sister was truly in shock. She looked like one of those figures in a wax museum, life like, but not real. When she found out, during our ceremony, that we had already legally married, two days before, she lost all of her color and roamed around afterwards in a sort of coma.

Mom and Dad were thrilled with the surprise wedding, but Peggy explained that the reason they weren't as shocked as she was, was because they had eloped themselves and they understood the excitement of such a secret.

Peggy said later, "There are only a few life-altering-type occasions. I mean, you're born, you marry, you give birth and you die! None of those events should come as a surprise to the people closest to you." It took her three days to process the information and stop being mad at me, and I have promised her that I will never surprise her again.

Over the last ten years of my singleness, I had become quite, no, ENTIRELY self-sufficient. One day when my sister and I were returning from a business trip, and she was going on about how much she missed her husband, I said, "No, thanks! Just give me a basset hound that's potty trained and that's all the company I need."

I don't think anyone can explain what it's like to be happily married to someone who has never been. I am surrounded by happy couples. My parents reek of bliss, and they have been married for 48 years. Peggy and Danny have had a beautiful relationship for two decades; our assistant, Dee Anne, has a great long-time marriage; our editor, Sydney, has been happy with her husband forever, and yet no one could explain to me what a happy marriage feels like. Even though I have been very close to all of them, somehow what they have, evaded me.

When I was fifteen, my dog, Emmy (a small generic, mop-like animal), ate an entire giant-size Hershey bar while we were out. (Mom had left it on the coffee table and Em just couldn't resist.) She became very ill.

I remember suffering right along with her, as she struggled like a beached, pregnant whale. She moaned as her tummy tried to digest the effects of her chocolate pig-out.

I thought, at the time, that the love I felt for that dog

had to be what it must feel like to be a mother. I thought, if she died, I would also cease to live!

When my first child was born, I remembered how I had felt about Emmy and was amused that, in my innocence, I had thought the two loves could be compared. One really was "puppy love."

When Mike was born, I felt a love that I could not explain. A spiritual love that transcends words. It was such a shock to experience that depth of love. Only another mother can know what an incredible feeling that is!

Now I can see why being happily married can't be explained. It's like the new mother feeling! It just has to be experienced.

I wouldn't trade my past for anything, because if I hadn't gone through a bad marriage, I don't think I would appreciate what I have now, as much as I do. It was definitely worth the ten-year wait to re-find this man. He has filled a void I didn't know existed. He has softened me and helped me to heal from the anger that has lurked in the potholes of my mind, just waiting to strike when least expected. (He went through an entire year of being blamed for the negative experiences I had in my first marriage and with other men I have loved.)

As I write this, I have only been married for a month, so my experience as a happily married woman is brief. However, Terry's and my outlook on life are the same, making our future pleasantly predictable. He loves life and, as long as I have known him, he has had a positive attitude. He is quick to admit he is wrong, and slow to blame. He makes me laugh and loves to please me. I have never known what it is to love a man the way I love Terry.

If you are happily married, take time out to be thankful for your mate and take a little extra time to pray for all of the single parents who don't have the blessing of a good husband. I hope God blesses your marriage and that your home is filled with love, laughter and kindness.

After reading this chapter, Peggy said that a person who is still on her honeymoon is too gooey to be real, and that we would be remiss if we didn't include in this chapter about marriage a paragraph or two about fighting. Sort of a "what-they-don't-teach-in-home-ec" side to everyday wedded bliss.

We think that there are probably about five basic fights married couples engage in, and should be warned of, before they put rings on each other. Maybe before the lovers could apply for the marriage license, they should have to pass a few tests besides the blood one.

For instance, we think that the bride-and groom-to-be should spend a night together before the nuptials, not to see if they are compatible sexually, but to see if the man goes to the bathroom in the middle of the night and leaves the toilet seat up!

According to a recent survey we took, 77.5% of the men we polled leave the seat up. In the wee hours, his spouse (if he has one) gets up, leaves the lights off so that she will not disturb her sleeping family (because if they wake up, they might want something), Brailles her way to the bathroom, goes to sit down and falls in! Because a standard toilet seat is approximately two inches thick, the woman is shocked to plunge past her expected target; and whiplash is a common injury!

There is a solution to this heinous male habit. Since it is virtually impossible to get a man to spend 15 minutes a day standing in the bathroom, saying, "Seat up! Seat down! Seat up! Seat down!" we have a better way. It's inexpensive and it could save medical and psychological bills and legal fees, down the road.

Just before bed, take plastic wrap and stretch it tightly over the toilet bowl. When he uses the facility, he'll wet all over himself and then he'll know what it feels like to go back to bed in wet pajamas! (Note to reader: This was Pam's solution and, remember, she's on her second marriage, so consider the possible ramifications of this particular hint.)

Another common fight occurs on an outing, in a car on a major highway. (This test should take place on either an L.A. or Boston freeway, going at least 65 miles per hour.) The couple must get lost, at which time the male will probably throw a map at the female and growl, "Where are we?" That same survey we conducted revealed that every man expects his mate to be a natural navigator. We, personally, can only read a map if the car and the map are going in the same direction! Men get nuts when they see a woman turn a map upside-down or sideways and then have trouble reading the words. If women would consent to motoring north only, they would never be confronted with this situation, and this common fight could be scratched off of the list.

With all of our newfangled technology, another fight has emerged. The "clicker" fight. Men need to learn that, just because they hold the remote control to the TV, they do not get to run the world. Men seem to be more global when it comes to watching television. They are capable of watching eight programs at once. We're not sure that they can actually keep track of what's going on, but they really don't seem to care. We think that most men should lose their clicker privileges until they are willing to share control with their wives.

What if every happy couple had to park an RV or launch a boat before they could tie the knot? There is not one male we know who is any fun when he's trying to back a trailer into a slot or maneuver a boat into its slip. Take extreme caution when considering the purchase of a boat or trailer because, in the name of recreation, one could end up in divorce court.

Since the state of Washington doesn't require premarital test fighting, Terry and I are ignorant of what may lie ahead.

Chapter Ten

A Mother's Day That Really Was

From Peggy:

A few days before Mother's Day, Danny said to me, "This year we're going to do something different for Mother's Day! We're not gonna go out for dinner and stand in those long lines, waiting for a table, like we do every year." I stared at him suspiciously. Surely he wouldn't DARE suggest that I prepare the meal! So what did he have in mind? "I'm going to take care of the dinner myself," he boasted. My suspicion turned to concern.

Danny is not renowned as a chef. Over the last year he had learned a few basics, but a galloping gourmet he was not! True, he'd made great strides since that first Saturday breakfast he'd fixed and brought to me on a tray, a few months back. I had been given hot coffee and a bowl of chili with onions and cheese sprinkled on top. (My niece, Joanna, was spending the weekend with us and later she told her mom, "There's no place like Aunt Peg's on a Sunday, but you never want to be there on Saturday!")

Being careful not to show my true feelings, which I feared would discourage Danny's efforts, I was falsely delighted with the breakfast. "Mmmm...chili...with onions too...I'll bet this'll hit the spot!"

"Yeah, I couldn't control the onion very well, though, so some of the chunks might be a little too big. How do you keep it from rolling around while you're chopping at it?"

Now, just a year later, he was a chop-o-matician. He'd learned the correct way to chop onions, slice mushrooms, cut potatoes, dice tomatoes and cube cheese; but prepare a whole dinner? No.

"Really? You're going to do the whole thing yourself? How special."

"No, I don't think I'll do it all myself. I'll make it a potluck. I'll call my dad, and your dad, and Terry, and get them to bring something for filler, but I'll do the main dish."

"Filler?"

"Yeah, you know, baked beans and stuff."

"Mmmm....baked beans and stuff....I'll bet that'll hit the spot!"

"I'll call everybody and set it up. You won't have to lift a finger." Danny called the greenhorn trio and each one agreed to bring the assigned "filler." Meanwhile, I made three follow-up calls to the mothers. I asked them to refrain from taking over, even if the food contribution was an embarrassment. The women agreed to sit back and let the men culinate.

Terry was to be the baked-bean man, but he hit a snag at the grocery store, trying to pick out dry beans that were the "right color." He called Pam for help. "The brown ones say 'kidney beans,' but aren't those what you get at a salad bar?" My sister advised him to go to the canned goods section (he knew the aisle number) and pick up a couple cans of B&M and "doctor" them with just the right blend of sauteed onions, crumbled bacon, Worchestershire, Grey Poupon, garlic and chili powder. He seemed semi-relieved.

Dad was in charge of providing the salad, and as a pleasant twist, he chose a recipe for a tropical fruit festival, the makings of which cost about thirty-five dollars. He elected to peel, pit and prepare the fruit the night before (a decision that Mom turned the other cheek to). Reading from the red-checkered cookbook, Dad was at an impasse, "Mom, where do we keep the bias?" "What?" "The bias, where is it? I'm supposed to cut this kiwi on the bias."

Danny's dad was assigned the dessert. He "U-picked" and finely sliced an entire flat of strawberries, purchased those packaged, yellow styrofoam-like shortcake replicas and a spray can of aircream, and he was ready for the party!

The Mother's Day celebration was to commence at 2:00 p.m. on Sunday. At noon, Danny (the "entree" preneur) was still chaised out with his morning paper. As the stove's digital advanced, I couldn't stand it any longer! I didn't smell anything cooking, the table hadn't been set, hors d'oeuvres were non-existent, and I caved.

"So, Babe, what're you going to serve for the main dish?"

"I don't know....I thought I'd go to the Food Pavilion and see what looks good."

"Mmmm....That should work."

"Yeah. Maybe I'll do a chicken."

"Uh huh. Chicken's always good."

"Yeah. Do you have a recipe for that Veal Pavarotti stuff you make?"

"Veal Scallopini?"

"Yeah."

"Gee, Babe, do you really want to get that involved? It's past noon."

"Nah, I better not chance it. I guess I'll barbecue."

"Uh huh. Good idea. You might want to be gettin' over to that Food Pavilion pretty soon now. I think you're gonna be losin' your light here before too long."

"Yeah, I'd better get my shower and head out."

I was a nervous wreck! Danny seemed oblivious to the fact that, in less than two hours, fourteen people would be sitting down to a blank table.

Returning from the store with an assortment of chicken

parts, he went to work. He carefully scrubbed each one, as if preparing it for surgery. He made barbecue "dip." He said that he didn't want sauce; he wanted to dip the parts in the stuff, not paint them with a brush. I explained that the recipe would be the same, whether he dipped or painted. He was pleased.

He took the raw chicken outside to the cold Weber as if he expected to turn a knob, like on the stove, and the coals would be glowing. He brought the chicken back into the house and asked me where I kept the charcoal lighter fluid. The next time I looked outside, flames were high above the grill, threatening to torch the bill of Danny's baseball cap, and Danny was standing back, with new respect for the container of Squeeze-A-Flame. I had to look away.

It was two o'clock. With singed eyebrows and red cheeks, Danny greeted the hungry guests. The proud culinarians carried their efforts to the kitchen, like 4-H-ers bringing their entries to the fair. Each one eyed the other's exhibit, anxious for the judging to begin; but I reminded them that we couldn't eat until the table was set. They looked disappointed.

I turned to the other mothers and asked them if they would like to join me in a game of pool while the men set their table. Although pool is nothing any of us would ever want to play, they all accepted the invitation.

Downstairs at the pool table, we realized that no one knew the rules, so we made them up. We called the game, "ball in the pants," and it went something like this: We would all use the same pole and take turns hitting whichever ball looked good. If the ball went into one of the pockets, the hitter had to take it out and put it in one of her own pockets. If her pockets were full, she could put the ball any place in her clothing as long as it would stay there without dropping. (Mom got to put two balls in her bra because her pockets were full.) We were having a great time, when Danny announced over the intercom, "Come on, everybody, dinner's on the table!"

"Okay," my sister lilted, "We'll be up as soon as the game is over." I covered my mouth to keep the gasp from trans-mitting into the kitchen, and we all got hysterical at the thought of turning the tables on our mates.

The table was set! The guests of honor had special plates, covered with shiny aluminum foil. (I learned later that the purpose of the foil was more functional than decorative. It was to save the men from having to wash our dishes!)

We each took our places at the feast table. Everything looked delicious! We were quite amazed. In their prepara-tions, the men had only neglected one small thing...the children.

"Mmmm, looks real good, Dad. Where are <u>we</u> gonna eat?" Chris looked around for more plates.

Danny grabbed a stack of paper plates for the six starv-ing outcasts and let them serve themselves, from our table. Reaching over the seated guests to fill their wobbly plates, they seemed like partakers of a hot meal at a mission. They took their pitiful portions and went off somewhere to eat by themselves.

The meal was delicious! The proud men traded recipes and watched to see whose dish was the most popular. When we were finished eating, I said, "Great dinner, Babe! How 'bout another game of ball in the pants, ladies?"

We left the men to their kitchen cleanup and retired to the family room. We found it interesting how fast they were able to finish their work. They didn't chat or nibble on leftovers; <u>they cleaned</u>. They were janitorial teammates, there to do a nasty job and do it fast!

There was only one casualty that wonderful Mother's Day...my ceramic turkey platter. (Danny had put the barbecued chicken on it and put it in a 400 degree oven to stay warm while he set the table.) We don't know how the men will outdo themselves next year, but we're going to let them try!

Afterword

From Pam:

Many of our homes are on shaky ground today. It seems that a lot of families use their houses like a person on a business trip uses a hotel. It's just a place where you check in, grab a bite to eat, see what's on T.V., use the phone a couple of times, set the alarm for the next morning, lock the door and go to bed.

A recent survey revealed that a married couple shares about four minutes of quality time daily with each other. It's no wonder the divorce courts are full of unhappy couples. Emerson said, "If a man wishes to acquaint himself with the spirit of the age, he must not go first to the state-house or the court-room. The subtle spirit of life must be sought in facts nearer. It is what is done and suffered in the house, that has the profoundest interest for us."

We can all have happier homes, but in order to do that, we've got to spend more time with each other. Cher, told

Barbara Walters, in an interview, "Life is not a dress rehearsal". We can't go back and reclaim time to spend with the people we love, but we can start today, making an effort to spend more time with them, in the future. That extra time, which you want more than anything, will be yours as soon as your family realizes, along with you, that it translates into fun, relaxation, appreciation, moral support and all the good things a family can offer each member. That's why you read this book.

You may think that there is too much to change to get the cooperation that you need and want; that to make your home what you picture in your mind, would take a miracle! There is no better place for a miracle to take place than in YOUR home!

Whenever Jesus performed a miracle, he started his prayer with thanksgiving. He had such conviction that the miracle was going to take place, that he would actually give thanks for it BEFORE the miracle was visible to the person receiving the healing.

Appreciation is a tricky thing to have. I read about a lady who had a kidney transplant, and for the first time in her adult life, she said that she felt good. She told that every day was a miracle to her. She cherished every moment with her husband and new baby daughter (who was able to grow to full term because of the transplant). The article said that she took time to delight in the smell of snow in the winter wind, to savor the taste of spring in a strawberry, to recognize the warmth of sun on her back. She relished the touch of her baby's satin skin, prized the color in even a cloudy day and treasured the sound of the voices of her family.

Just before I read the article about this lady, I had gone on a rampage of complaints. Somebody's stereo was too loud, my new perm made me look like Gene Shallot. The ailing garbage disposal had just chewed it's last potato peel and Chelsea Mariehad come in the house, thrilled with the new odor she toted from rolling in something very old and dead. I thought, why is it that I don't savor my life the way that lady does? Would I have to be hooked up to a dialysis machine for twenty years to appreciate my kidneys? Would I have to lose my sight, my tongue, my hair or my house to appreciate them?

I heard that Jesus healed ten lepers and only one came back to thank him. I wonder if I would have been that grateful one, or would I have gone off, merrily on my way, with "secret appreciation" that would have only lasted until I got busy into some project? I'm afraid, when I look at my track record in this life, I would have been one of the other nine.

If a fashion model with a gorgeous complexion had a pimple on her cheek, most of us would zero in on the blemish immediately. If the identical size of the pimple was now a clear spot, and that small clear spot was put on the cheek of an acne infected teenager, we would never notice that healthy spot. With no effort, we see what is wrong much more than we see what is right.

You have the power to change the climate in your home. Start today by appreciating the fact that you have a family. Start seeing the miracle as if it has already happened. When you close this book be thankful that it wasn't in Braille. When you get up out of your chair, give thanks to your legs, your feet and your hands. Also give thanks that you are in a position to change the world, because you have the ability to change your home for the better.

From Peggy:

It was 7:00 am when the phone rang. I thought it was Annette wondering which shoes and outfit Allyson was going to wear to school. The voice on the other end was familiar, but in a strange sort of way. It was shivery and higher pitched than usual. It was my mother.

"Peg, come quick it's Dad!"

"We'll be right there!"

I hung up the phone, not knowing WHAT it was about my dad. Five years earlier we'd been through the experience of his heart attack, followed by quadruple by-pass surgery. I was afraid we might not get there in time. I tried to breath my way out of the sick feeling I had.

My parent's house is about six miles away. Danny drove so fast that it seemed as if most of the time we were going sideways. He maneuvered through the tangled morning traffic with the confidence of a weathered policeman going to an emergency.

"Are you okay?"

"Yeah, just shaky."

We didn't say anything more. Danny was darting around the motorized stumbling blocks in our path (their drivers ignorant of our problem) as if he had the privilege of a flashing blue light on top of our Suburban. Every traffic light seemed to be against us. We were slowed by a cluster of children in a school zone and stalled by the bumper-to-bumper commuters on the freeway. All I could think about was my dad. *'Just let him still be here.'* I prayed. *'I want to be able to tell him I love him.'* As much as I wanted to talk to Dad again, I had no regrets. There wasn't anything I needed to forgive or be forgiven for. There were no misunderstand-

196

ings, no hard feelings, no concerns for his eternity...just love. He and Mom had spent the past weekend with our kids while Danny and I were away. It had been more of a party than a responsibility. They'd played cards and talked and laughed from the time we'd left. Jeff had said, "Mom, Papa is the nicest person I've ever met in my life."

"Nicer than I am?"

"Papa is the nicest person I've ever met in my life."

Mom and Dad had shared a wonderful 48 years of love. She was the person I was worried about. How could two who had become so completely one, be separated?

We couldn't get into the driveway because of the ambulance and emergency rescue trucks. Danny stopped alongside the street, partially blocking one lane of traffic and we bolted from the truck. A paramedic was coming out of the front door. His face told nothing. I stopped squarely in front of him and forced him to answer my question, "Is he all right?" The same blank expression became audible. "He's fine." For an instant I wanted to shake some emotion into him. I wanted to say, "That's my father you're talking about! I thought he might be gone! Where's your sensitivity?"

Inside the front door, we found enough sensitivity to make up for the poor man outside who had, somewhere along the way, lost his. Paramedics were gathered around my 73-year-old father. They were kind, careful and comforting as they listened to my dad explain what he thought had happened.

He had fainted and Mom had not been able to bring him out of it. Later she told us, "I just kept petting him and telling him, 'Don't do this Dad! God loves you! Come on Dad, don't do it!'"

Dad was irritated by the commotion he had caused. Pam (barefoot and in a nightgown and robe) and Terry (dressed in the night-before's sport shirt and handy, but wrinkled slacks) had leaped out of bed at Mom's beckoning and, living only blocks away, got there as Dad started to come back to consciousness. By the time we got there, Dad was totally coherent, but a bit confused by the presence of the entire family.

"What are you guys doing here?"

"Oh we just wondered what you folks were doing this morning."

Everybody laughed and the humor seemed to ease the tension.

We all (except for Dad, who argued that he was just fine) agreed that because of his medical history, he should go to the hospital and be checked. It was November 8, election day. As the paramedics hoisted their slightly-less-than-passive patient onto the gurney, my father had come back to himself.

"Are you guys Republicans or Democrats?"

"Does the name Dukakis mean anything to you?"

"Yeah, isn't he the guy who says he smells victory? I think he's smelling something else!"

"I don't know, they say it's gonna be close."

"Oh, now I get it. You guys go all over town picking up Republicans today so we can't vote!"

He was back to life.

Mom and Danny and I followed the ambulance in the truck. Pam and Terry came a few minutes and clothes and shoes later.

On the way, we all felt spared. Spared the pain of

separation; spared the tough decisions; spared the tears and grief of giving up someone we all love.

The emergency was over. We were told by the doctor that everything was fine. Just to be sure, we wanted Dad to be checked out thoroughly. We insisted that he stay in the hospital overnight.

On the way back home that evening, Mom said, "How would you like a house guest tonight sweet Dan?"

"What's in it for me Dolores?"

"I won't call you in the middle of the night because I hear prowlers. It'll save you a trip."

"Sounds good to me!"

I sat between them in the front seat. My arm was through my mother's. She and Danny were playing their favorite game of pitching mother-in-law one liners back and forth like a sketch out of an old Carol Burnett show. They laughed as she threatened to move in permanently and he said he'd welcome having a housekeeper even if she was a little old.

I looked at my mother's hand, resting on top of mine. It looked like my own, only it was smaller and speckly. It had obviously worked a few years longer than mine. Her nicked but polished wedding band was evidence of a commitment she'd made to my father almost a half century earlier.

I looked at my own wedding ring. Would Danny and I have the good fortune to enjoy each other's company another twenty or thirty years? With a job like his, even though he wears a bulletproof vest, there are no guarantees that he'll come home safely at the end of each day. I wondered if we would be married as long as my parents had been.

I thought about how fragile this physical life is. You can blink your eyes and it's gone. That tangible presence that means so much to your own life, and yet can't be held or saved a second beyond its time. I thought about being kinder to Danny. I thought about not making a big deal over little things, as I so often seem to do.

Somehow the issue of who makes the bed, turns into foolish, petty nonsense when you remember what a blessing it is to have a wonderful mate. A person to mutually respect and inspire. One to laugh with and confide in. Someone to share the crises as well as the exhilaration. If he were gone....how you would ache to have him back. You surely wouldn't quibble over things that didn't really matter.

Deep feelings of gratitude came to me, riding home from the hospital that day. I was remembering what's important in life.

I didn't want this book to end without an after thought. It's wonderful to have a mate who shares the housework, but it's more wonderful to share life with someone you love.

What a naughty title we gave this book, "I'm OK...But You Have A Lot Of Work To Do!" I think I'll work on not being so self-righteous.

God bless your home and family!

Love,

Sam & Peggy

Appendix

NEW HOUSE RULES

- IF IT'S NOT DECORATIVE PUT IT AWAY
- NO DISHES IN THE SINK
- PUT TOILET SEATS DOWN
- NO LAUNDRY IN BEDROOMS
- ONE HOUR GRACE ON PERSONAL BELONGINGS
- NO TOOTHPASTE IN SINK
- SORT PERSONAL LAUNDRY
- REPLACE TOILET PAPER ROLL
- NO DISHES IN BEDROOMS
- NO TUB RINGS
- LAST ONE OUT OF BED MAKES IT
- NO WHISKERS IN SINK

HAVE A NICE DAY!

INFRACTION CARD FOR		
DATE	**INFRACTION**	**BALANCE**
	*TOTAL*_____	

POINT CHART FOR :

DATE	ACTIVITY (JOB)	VALUE	BALANCE FORWARD	√

DAILY   **30 MINUTES**

Prepare Meals

To make clean up easier, put utensils and mixing bowls in the
dishwasher and soak pots and pans. Clear counters before
eating.

NOTE: Don't forget to defrost!

♥   **KITCHEN**

DAILY   **30 MINUTES**

1] Empty Dishwasher, Set Table   [5 Min.]
2] Fill Dishwasher [*]
3] Pots, Pans, Serving Dishes   [10 Min.]
4] Clean Countertops, Surfaces   [5 Min.]
5] Scour Sink, Empty Garbage   [5 Min.]
6] Sweep Floor, Shake Rugs   [5 Min.]

* INFRACTION PENALTY!
♥   **KITCHEN**

WEEKLY/EVERY OTHER WEEK   **[ONE HOUR]**

1] Wash Window Over Sink   [5 Min.]
2] Clean Refrigerator   [10 Min.]
3] Clean Microwave   [3 Min.]
4] Clean Range Top   [5 Min.]
5] Wash Floor   [15 Min.]
6] Wax Floor   [15 Min.]
7] Self-Cleaning Oven   [5 Min.]
8] Wash Scatter Rugs   [2 Min.]
Note: If this cleaning is done weekly, the times will be accurate. If it is
skipped for more than one or two weeks, it will take longer.
♥   **KITCHEN**

204

MONTHLY/   **[15 MINUTES]**
EVERY OTHER MONTH

1]   Wash Canisters & KnicKnacks   [5 Min.]
2]   Clean Cutting board   [5 Min.]
3]   Clean Small Appliances   [5 Min.]

LAST DONE _____   SKIPPED _____

♥   **KITCHEN**

SEASONALLY   **[ONE HOUR]**

1]   Clean Light fixtures   [30 Min.]
2]   Clean Stove Fan, Filter, Hood   [30 Min.]

LAST DONE _____   SKIPPED _____

♥   **KITCHEN**

TWICE YEARLY   **[ONE HOUR]**

Strip Old Wax   [60 Min.]

LAST DONE _____   SKIPPED _____

♥   **KITCHEN**

TWICE YEARLY/   **[ONE HOUR]**
YEARLY

    Clean & Reorganize Pantry   [60 Min.]

LAST DONE _____   SKIPPED_____

♥   **KITCHEN**

TWICE YEARLY/   **[ONE HOUR]**
YEARLY

    Clean & Reorganize Cupboards   [60 Min.]

LAST DONE_____   SKIPPED _____

♥   **KITCHEN**

TWICE YEARLY/   **[ONE HOUR]**
YEARLY

    Clean & Reorganize Drawers   [60 Min.]

LAST DONE _____   SKIPPED _____

♥   **KITCHEN**

TWICE YEARLY/   [ONE HOUR]
YEARLY

    Wash & Iron Curtains   [60 Min.]

LAST DONE _____   SKIPPED _____

♥   KITCHEN

TWICE YEARLY/   [ONE HOUR]
YEARLY

    Wash & Polish Woodwork   [60 Min.]

LAST DONE_____   SKIPPED _____

♥   KITCHEN

YEARLY   [ONE HOUR]

1] Defrost Freezer   [55 Min.]
2] Clean Drip Pan & Coils   [5 Min.]

LAST DONE _____   SKIPPED_____

♥   KITCHEN

WEEKLY/EVERY OTHER WEEK   [45 MINUTES]

1]	Clean Toilet*	[5 Min.]
2]	Clean Tub*	[5 Min.]
3]	Scour Sink*	[5 Min.]
4]	Clean Shower Stall	[5 Min.]
5]	Clean Mirror*	[1 Min.]
6]	Polish Counters	[2 Min.]
7]	Wash Floor	[10 Min.]
8]	Wax Floor	[10 Min.]
9]	Wash Scatter Rug	[2 Min.]

* Infraction penalty for tub ring, dirty sink or spattered mirror. Also penalty for towels, toiletries, small appliances, and any personal belongings left out. Count infractions for an empty toilet paper roll, toilet seat left up or the light left on.

♥   **BATHROOM**

**TWICE YEARLY/
YEARLY   [ONE HOUR]**

     Wash & Iron Curtains   [60 Min.]

LAST DONE _____   SKIPPED _____

♥   **BATHROOM**

**TWICE YEARLY/
YEARLY   [ONE HOUR]**

     Strip Old Wax   [60 Min.]

LAST DONE_____   SKIPPED_____

♥   **BATHROOM**

208

```
┌─────────────────────────────────────────────────┐
│ SEASONALLY                        [ONE HOUR]      │
│                                                   │
│ 1]  Polish Woodwork                  [25 Min.]    │
│ 2]  Polish Tile                      [25 Min.]    │
│ 3]  Clean Light Fixture              [10 Min.]    │
│                                                   │
│ LAST DONE_____   SKIPPED _____    │
│ ♥                                  BATHROOM       │
└─────────────────────────────────────────────────┘
```

```
┌─────────────────────────────────────────────────┐
│ SEASONALLY                        [30 MINUTES]    │
│                                                   │
│    Clean & Reorganize Cupboards,                  │
│    Drawers & Medicine Cabinet        [30 Min.]    │
│                                                   │
│ LAST DONE _____   SKIPPED _____    │
│ ♥                                  BATHROOM       │
└─────────────────────────────────────────────────┘
```

```
┌─────────────────────────────────────────────────┐
│ DAILY                             [10 MINUTES]    │
│                                                   │
│ 1]  Make Bed*                        [ 5 Min.]    │
│ 2]  Put Clothes Away*                [ 3 Min.]    │
│ 3]  Laundry to Laundry Room          [ 1 Min.]    │
│ 4]  Dishes to Dishwasher*            [ 1 Min.]    │
│                                                   │
│ * Infraction Penalty!                             │
│                                                   │
│ NOTE: Because these jobs all carry an infraction  │
│ penalty, they will become automatic very quickly. │
│ ♥                                  BEDROOMS       │
└─────────────────────────────────────────────────┘
```

WEEKLY/   [15 MINUTES]
EVERY OTHER WEEK

1]   Change Sheets   [5 Min. Actual]
2]   Clean Under Bed   [5 Min.]
3]   Clean Mirror   [5 Min.]

LAST DONE _____   SKIPPED _____

♥   BEDROOMS

SEASONALLY   [ONE HOUR]

1]   Turn Mattress
2]   Wash Mattress Pad & Bedding   [5 Min.]
3]   Clean Closets & Drawers   [45 Min.]
4]   Clean Light Fixtures   [10 Min.]

LAST DONE _____   SKIPPED _____

♥   BEDROOMS

MONTHLY   [25 MINUTES]

1]   Wash Floor   [10 Min.]
2]   Wax Floor   [10 Min.]
3]   Polish Appliances   [5 Min.]

LAST DONE_____   SKIPPED _____

♥   LAUNDRY ROOM

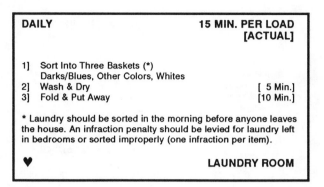

```
DAILY                          15 MIN. PER LOAD
                                    [ACTUAL]


1]   Sort Into Three Baskets (*)
     Darks/Blues, Other Colors, Whites
2]   Wash & Dry                        [ 5 Min.]
3]   Fold & Put Away                   [10 Min.]

* Laundry should be sorted in the morning before anyone leaves
the house. An infraction penalty should be levied for laundry left
in bedrooms or sorted improperly (one infraction per item).

♥                              LAUNDRY ROOM
```

```
DAILY                             [5 MINUTES]



     Feed & Clean Up After Pets        [ 5 Min.]



NOTE:  Children can be assigned odd or even days and can alter-
nate being responsible for pet care.

♥                              MISCELLANEOUS
```

```
DAILY                            [10 MINUTES]



     Sort & Answer Mail



NOTE: A quick note when you first think about it, is worth more
than the nice long letter you'll never have time to write.

♥                              MISCELLANEOUS
```

211

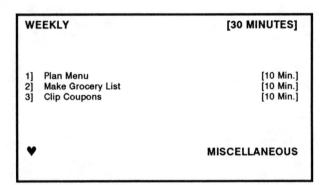

```
WEEKLY                           [30 MINUTES]


   1]   Plan Menu                     [10 Min.]
   2]   Make Grocery List             [10 Min.]
   3]   Clip Coupons                  [10 Min.]



   ♥                          MISCELLANEOUS
```

```
WEEKLY                            [ONE HOUR]


   1]   Miscellaneous Errands         [30 Min.]
   2]   Banking                       [10 Min.]
   3]   Post Office                   [10 Min.]
   4]   Dry Cleaners                  [10 Min.]



   ♥                          MISCELLANEOUS
```

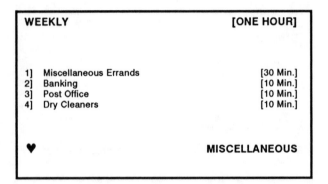

```
WEEKLY                            [ONE HOUR]


   1]   Grocery Shopping              [45 Min.]
   2]   Unpacking The Groceries       [15 Min.]



   ♥                          MISCELLANEOUS
```

```
WEEKLY                              [10 MINUTES]


1]  Change Kitty Litter              [ 5 Min.]
2]  Clean Bird (Hamster) Cage        [ 5 Min.]


LAST DONE_____   SKIPPED_____

♥                                MISCELLANEOUS
```

```
EVERY OTHER WEEK                    [30 MINUTES]


1]  Mending                          [10 Min.]
2]  Ironing                          [10 Min.]
3]  Hand Washables                   [10 Min.]


LAST DONE _____  SKIPPED _____
♥                                MISCELLANEOUS
```

```
WEEKLY/                             [ONE HOUR]
EVERY OTHER WEEK


    Wash Car & Clean Inside


NOTE: Don't waste your time, run it through Otto's Auto-wash

LAST DONE _____  SKIPPED _____

♥                                MISCELLANEOUS
```

DEPENDS ON SITUATION   **[ONE HOUR]**

Pay Bills   [60 Min.]

♥   **MISCELLANEOUS**

MONTHLY   **[15 MINUTES]**

Balance Checkbook With Bank Statement

NOTE: Keep a running balance in the checkbook at all times. Order checks that come with a carbon copy.

♥   **MISCELLANEOUS**

MONTHLY/   **[ONE HOUR]**
EVERY OTHER MONTH

1]   Polish Silver & Silverware   [30 Min.]
2]   Polish Copper, Brass, Etc.   [30 Min.]

LAST DONE_____   SKIPPED_____

♥   **MISCELLANEOUS**

214

**MONTHLY/   [ONE HOUR]
EVERY OTHER MONTH**

Clean Fireplaces(s)

LAST DONE _____   SKIPPED _____

♥   **THROUGHOUT**

SEASONALLY   [10 MINUTES]

Clean Furnace Vents

NOTE: Shake outside and wash in dishwasher.

LAST DONE_____   SKIPPED _____

♥   **MISCELLANEOUS**

SEASONALLY   [ALL DAY]

Wash Windows Inside & Out

NOTE: Professionals can do this job in half the time. Consider
how valuable **your** time is. Hire a professional.

LAST DONE_____   SKIPPED _____

♥   **MISCELLANEOUS**

EVERY OTHER YEAR

Have Drapes Cleaned
Living Room   Last Cleaned _____
Family Room   Last Cleaned _____
Dining Room   Last Cleaned _____
Master Bedroom   Last Cleaned _____
Bedroom   Last Cleaned _____
Bedroom   Last Cleaned _____
Other   Last Cleaned _____

Note: To avoid a huge cleaning bill, count the pairs and divide by 24 to spread the expense over the months.
♥   **MISCELLANEOUS**

WEEKLY/   **[ONE HOUR]**
EVERY OTHER WEEK

1] Vacuum   [30 Min.]
2] Dust & Polish Furniture   [30 Min.]

LAST DONE _____   SKIPPED _____

♥   **THROUGHOUT**

EVERY OTHER MONTH/   **[ONE HOUR]**
SEASONALLY

1] Cobwebs   [10 Min.]
2] High Places & Ledges   [10 Min.]
3] Light Switches   [5 Min.]
4] Telephones   [5 Min.]
5] Pictures   [5 Min.]
6] Lamp Shades   [5 Min.]
7] Blinds   [20 Min.]

♥   **THROUGHOUT**

TWICE YEARLY/   **[ALL DAY]**
YEARLY

Move Furniture
Shampoo Carpet

Note: Professional carpet cleaners will save you time and
money and they will do a better job.

LAST DONE _____   SKIPPED _____

♥   **THROUGHOUT**

IN SEASON   **[ONE HOUR]**
WEEKLY

Mow Lawn   **[60 Min.]**

NOTE: This is a good job to delegate to a teenager who needs
to earn points in exchange for the car keys.

♥   **OUTSIDE**

IN SEASON   **[TWO HOURS]**
WEEKLY/
EVERY OTHER WEEK

Clean & Weed Flower Beds
Rake Leaves

Miscellaneous Yard Care To Include:
Fertilizing, Weed Control, Trimming, Etc.

LAST DONE _____   SKIPPED _____

♥   **OUTSIDE**

WEEKLY/   **[30 MINUTES]**
EVERY OTHER WEEK

1]	Sweep/Spray Wash Patio	[10 Min.]
2]	Sweep/Spray Wash Porch	[10 Min.]
3]	Sweep/Spray Wash Walks	[10 Min.]

LAST DONE_____   SKIPPED _____

♥   **OUTSIDE**

TWICE YEARLY/   **[ONE HOUR]**
YEARLY

Clean The Eaves   [60 Min.]

LAST DONE_____   SKIPPED _____

♥   **OUTSIDE**

Pam and Peggy's Other Books

***Sidetracked Home Executives**...From Pigpen to Paradise.* Discusses how to change your attitude, improve your appearance, motivate your family, get rid of clutter in five weeks, be ready for Christmas by the first of December and how to use our 3x5 cardfile system that will organize your home forever.

The Sidetracked Sisters Catch-Up On The Kitchen. Menu planning made automatic, food shopping made speedy, storage made simple and sensible, and recipes rounded up for your convenience.

The Sidetracked Sisters' Happiness File. Solve your most pressing problems, use time you never knew you had, celebrate your family's living history, discover and develop your hidden assets and watch your happiness grow with a system that helps you remember the simple things that mean so much.

Pam and Peggy have entertained audiences nationwide. If your church, business or club is interested in one of their presentations, a short video tape is available upon request. Call **Sidetracked Home Executives, 1-206-696-4091**, for more information.

ORGANIZER KITS

Home Executive Kit. Sturdy plastic jumbo-sized 3x5 file box contains: printed index cards, detailed with job titles and descriptions (color coded for frequency), time estimates and Pam and Peggy's personal household hints; plus dividers 1-31, January-December, A-Z and four unlabeled $25.00

Kitchen Kit. Sturdy plastic jumbo-sized 3x5 file box contains: printed index cards detailed with job titles for kitchen maintenance (color coded for frequency), time estimates and Pam and Peggy's personal kitchen hints, favorite menus and recipes; plus dividers 1-31, A-Z and 15 labeled with specific categories................................$25.00

50/50 Family Kit. Sturdy plastic jumbo-sized 3x5 file box contains: printed index cards specifically designed for delegating to family members and/or a housekeeper, detailed with job titles, descriptions and time estimates; plus a set of 50 infraction cards (for keeping track of each family member's clutter violations), bright colored, adhesive infraction markers, and dividers 1-31, January-December and A-Z $25.00

PRINTED 3X5 CARDS

Home Executive Cards.   Printed index cards, detailed with job titles and descriptions (color coded for frequency), time estimates and Pam and Peggy's personal household hints... **$15.00**

Kitchen Cards.   Printed index cards detailed with job titles for kitchen maintenance (color coded for frequency), time estimates and Pam and Peggy's personal kitchen hints, favorite menus and recipes.................................. **$15.00**

50/50 Family Delegating Cards.   Printed index cards specifically designed for delegating to family members and/or a housekeeper, detailed with job titles, descriptions and time estimates, plus 50 infraction cards for keeping track of each family member's clutter violations.

.... **$15.00**

Infraction Cards.   Set of 50 printed index cards to keep track of each family member's clutter violations.

.... **$5.00**

31 Days of Inspiration.   Each card has a special message to give you encouragement and a positive thought for the day... **$5.00**

CASSETTE TAPES

__Home Organization Made Easy:__ Energized by an audience of more than a thousand women, these five, 60-minute cassette tapes present Pam and Peggy's complete, nationally-known program, which led them "from pigpen to paradise". Included in the original program, are steps on how to employ their 3x5 cardfile system to help you: figure out what you're doing and why, change your attitude and improve your appearance, conquer closet clutter, enlist family cooperation and move forward in a new direction. Book references are from *SIDETRACKED HOME EXECUTIVES* and *THE SIDETRACKED SISTERS CATCH-UP ON THE KITCHEN* $55.00

__Success and Happiness Workshop:__ Three 60-minute cassette tapes share Pam and Peggy's personal experiences in business. They describe how they turned challenges into opportunities and achieved success by making their goals a reality. Book references are from *THE SIDETRACKED SISTERS' HAPPINESS FILE* $35.00

__50/50 Family Workshop:__ Two 60-minute cassette tapes explain Pam and Peggy's overnight miracle solution to family clutter and lack of cooperation. Book references are from **I'M OK...BUT YOU HAVE A LOT OF WORK TO DO!**...$25.00

__Home for the Holidays:__ Two 60-minute cassette tapes, filled with inspiration, motivation and humor to help you celebrate the Christmas season, hassle-free...............$25.00

__Daily Inspiration:__ A 30-minute cassette tape designed to keep you on the right track with uplifting thoughts for the day $5.00

VIDEO TAPES

Home Organization Made Easy Video Workshop: Energized by an audience of more than a thousand women , these five, 60-minute (VHS) video tapes present Pam and Peggy's nationally-known program, which led them "from pigpen to paradise". Included in the original program are steps on how to employ their 3x5 cardfile system to help you: figure out what you are doing and why, change your attitude and improve your appearance, conquer closet clutter, enlist family cooperation and move forward in a new direction. Book references are from; *SIDETRACKED HOME EXECUTIVES* and *THE SIDETRACKED SISTERS CATCH-UP ON THE KITCHEN*.. $250.00

NEWSLETTER

She's On Track: Bi-monthly newsletter (one year subscription, six issues) filled with inspiration, humor and helpful homemaking hints to keep you "on track".

....$12.50 per year

ORDER FORM

NAME _____

ADDRESS _____

CITY, STATE_____ ZIP _____

PHONE (_____) _____

ITEM	COST	TOTAL
☐ ORGANIZER KITS		
☐ Home Executive Kit	$25.00	
☐ Kitchen Kit	$25.00	
☐ 50/50 Family Kit	$25.00	
PRINTED 3X5 CARDS		
☐ Home Executive Cards	$15.00	
☐ Kitchen Cards	$15.00	
☐ 50/50 Family Delegating Cards	$15.00	
☐ Infraction Cards	$5.00	
☐ 31 Days of Inspiration	$5.00	
CASSETTE TAPES		
☐ Home Organization Made Easy	$55.00	
☐ Success & Happiness Workshop	$35.00	
☐ 50/50 Family Workshop	$25.00	
☐ Home for the Holidays	$25.00	
☐ Daily Inspiration	$5.00	
VIDEO TAPES:		
☐ Home Organization Made Easy	$250.00	
NEWSLETTER:		
☐ She's on Track*	$12.50	
Postage & Handling (*except on Newsletter subscriptions)	$3.00	
Subtotal		
Sales Tax (Wa. residents only 7.3%)		
All orders outside USA add $4.00		
TOTAL ENCLOSED (US funds only please)		

Bank Card Orders (check one):   ( ) VISA   ( ) MASTERCARD

Bank Card No. _ _ _ _ _ _ _ _ _ _ _ _ _ _ _ _

Expiration Date:_____   Please allow 4-6 weeks for delivery

RUSH ORDERS WITH VISA OR MASTERCARD: *1 (206) 696-4091*

Send to: **SIDETRACKED HOME EXECUTIVES**

401 NW Overlook Dr.

Vancouver, WA 98665